THE IMPORTANCE OF BEING OSCAR

The Wit and Wisdom of Oscar Wilde
Set Against His Life and Times

Leslie Frewin

W.H. ALLEN · LONDON
1986

Printed and bound in Great Britain by
The Garden City Press Ltd, Letchworth, Herts SG6 1JS
for the Publishers, W. H. Allen & Co. Plc
44 Hill Street, London W1X 8LB

ISBN 0 491 03185 8

To the memory of my friend

MICHÉAL MAC LIAMMÓIR

that other genius of the theatre who knew far better than I the importance of being Oscar.

Humanity takes itself too seriously.
It is the world's original sin. If
the caveman had known how to laugh,
history would have been different.

—OSCAR WILDE (1854-1900)

If, with the literate, I am
Impelled to try an epigram,
I never seek to take the credit—
We all assume that Oscar said it!

—DOROTHY PARKER (1893-1967)

One cannot define in a sentence
a man whom it has taken God
several millions of years to make!

—ARTHUR RANSOME (1884-1967)

CONTENTS

PROLOGUE

Wit is so shining a quality that everybody admires it; most people aim at it, all people fear it, and few love it, unless in themselves.
— LORD CHESTERFIELD
Letters to My Godson
18 December 1765

The truth of Oscar Wilde's words were arrogantly prophetic when he said, "Somehow or other I'll be famous, and if not famous, I'll be notorious." Within a few years, his intellectual brilliance, writing talent, and acerbic wit had propelled him from obscurity into dominance of the salons of the literary intelligentsia.

Even when he was sixteen, his repartee was masterly. At his first ball at Dublin Castle, not without courage he asked one of Ireland's most formidable unmarried titled ladies to dance. Looking disdainfully through her lorgnette at the assured youth who stood before her, she said, derisively, "Do you think I'm going to dance with a child?" Although a mere boy, Wilde, with ready wit and a faint suggestion of mock courtesy, replied, "Madam, if I had known you were in that condition, I would never have asked you!"

This book, drawn from conversations and criticism, his plays, poetry, fairy stories, footnotes, prefaces, *feuilletons*, letters, speeches, essays, articles, pronouncements, and theatrical dialogue, reveals Oscar Wilde's many-faceted character and mordant wit. There can be no question as to his genius. He bestrode the glittering social and literary stage of his time (albeit stealthily), stalked, as in many of the Greek plays so beloved by him, by the shadow of tragedy. After the sensational and contumacious Trials, he wrote with penetrating truth, "All trials are trials for one's life, and all sentences are sentences of death."

Yet there was a warmer, happier side to the vital genius of Wilde—a side that revealed the Lover of Life, the Prince of Gaiety, the Lord of Laughter. His audacious imagination and wit, unparalleled powers of coruscating conversation, his infectious sense of fun, his incomparable plays, books, and criticism—all fairly dominated the theatricality of the social plateau of a swaggering age of literary giants: Hardy, James, Edmund Gosse, Wells, Browning, Swinburne, Moore, Hall Caine, Shaw, Frank Harris, the Webbs, Housman, Conan Doyle, Barrie, Dean Inge, Yeats, Kipling, Bennett, Belloc, Davies, Synge, Max Beerbohm, Ford Madox Ford, de la Mare, and Chesterton, among a host of writing and allied talents. In the role of supreme master of the language of laughter, Oscar Wilde towered above them all; many matched his success, but none matched his wit.

Author of an unrelenting torrent of aphorisms, epithets, maxims, epigrams, paradoxes, quotes, asides, ad-libs, cut-and-thrust exchanges, bons mots, scintillating repartee, barbs, and satirical sayings, his craftsmanship and iconoclasm changed the tempo of his times. His literary output during the ten years in which he produced his major works brought him a decade of dazzling success.

Like other gifted artists, he was frequently in a state of

near-penury. But even the experience of that unhappy condition could and did produce a Wildean golden nugget—this with wry humour: "It is sad. One half of the world does not believe in God, and other half does not believe in me!"

He shocked and spellbound his audiences and intimates, astounding them with his prodigious academic knowledge and biting perception. His charismatic and compelling personality captivated literati and *longueurs* alike. Some idea of his achievement is listed at the end of this book. What is *not* listed, but what I hope is inherent in these pages, is a variegated evocation of his irreverent eccentricities, his humourously affected *hauteur*, his boundless kindness, and his infinite capacity as an unassailably gifted *bon vivant*.

Wilde's decade of creativity produced an abundance of fine writing: *The Happy Prince and Other Stories; Lord Arthur Savile's Crime;* a further enchanting book of "fairy stories," *A House of Pomegranates;* and his book of four essays, *Intentions*, published in 1891, followed in the same year by his strange, controversial novel, *The Picture of Dorian Gray*, a book that scandalized Victorians, as well he knew it would! Of his plays, in their genre, there is but one adjective to describe *Lady Windermere's Fan, A Woman of No Importance, An Ideal Husband, The Importance of Being Earnest*—incomparable!

His tender, evocative poetry provided further landmarks in a career of accomplishment, not to mention his incisive book reviews, essays, and other articles. His political tracts, notably *The Soul of Man Under Socialism*, were enervated by polished wit and devilishly splendid dissertations on contemporary society and the way it would go, not merely the way it was going. Read it again, written as it was in the late 1890s, and relate it to life today!

Even his countless letters to the press reveal an artist who dominated the language of his adopted country. He once said,

"The longer one studies life and literature, the more strongly one feels that behind everything that is wonderful stands the individual, and that it is not the moment that makes the man but the man who creates the age." As far as he was concerned, it was a faultless assertion.

Was Wilde, the man and writer who single-handedly created "The Wildean Age," ahead of his time? There is little doubt that he was. Had he lived and worked a hundred years later, it is equally certain that, instead of being consigned to disgrace and obloquy, he would have been showered with honors and awards; a British peerage would have been no less than his due, if not the loftier Order of Merit. But he lived and worked in the cant-ridden, bigoted era of the Victorian age which would never openly admit the veracity of Mrs. Patrick Campbell's engaging advice, "I don't care what you do as long as you don't do it in the streets and frighten the horses!"

That Wilde had an imbalanced sexual streak in his nature is today acknowledged by most. Yet strangely it was an imbalance of which neither his devoted wife, Constance, nor his family and close friends were aware. Even Shaw admits that he was totally ignorant of its existence. But does not history record a succession of the world's great artistic talents who suffered a like imbalance? As W. T. Stead, the crusading editor and journalist who had vigorously exposed child prostitution in Victorian London, said when he heard of Wilde's arrest, "If all the persons guilty of Oscar Wilde's (alleged) offences were to be clapped into jail, there would be a very surprising exodus from Eton and Harrow, Rugby and Winchester, and similar British public schools!"

Wilde's mistake, of course, was to seek to *defend* himself against the vicious calumny of the "Black Marquis"—Lord Queensbury. Even in the last part of the twentieth century, iniquitous elements of the hypocrisy of Victorian England linger still—hypocrisy that was never more graphically measured

nor more effectively attacked than by Lord Macaulay in his
Essay on Thomas Moore's Letters and Journals of Lord Byron,
published in June 1831, some twenty-three years before Wilde
was born. Ponder a moment on the words of that perspica-
cious literary peer:

> We know of no spectacle so ridiculous as the British public in
> one of its periodical fits of morality. In general, elopements,
> divorces and family quarrels pass with little notice. We read
> the scandal, talk about it for a day, and forget it. But once in
> six or seven years our virtue becomes outrageous. We cannot
> suffer the laws of religion and decency to be violated. We must
> take a stand against vice. We must teach libertines that the
> English people appreciate the importance of domestic ties. Ac-
> cordingly, some unfortunate man, in no respect more depraved
> than hundreds whose offences have been treated with leniency,
> is singled out as an expiatory sacrifice. If he has children, they
> are taken from him. If he has a profession, he has to be driven
> from it. He is cut by the higher orders, and hissed by the lower.
> He is, in truth, a sort of whipping-boy, by whose vicarious
> agonies all the other transgressors of the same class are, it is
> supposed, sufficiently chastised. We reflect very complacently
> on our own severity, and compare with great pride the high
> standard of morals established in England with the Parisian
> laxity. At length our anger is satiated. Our victim is ruined and
> heart-broken. And our virtue goes quickly to sleep for seven
> years more.

No doubt Oscar Wilde well knew Macaulay's words, for he
was nothing if not an enemy of cant. He must have known,
too, of the Countess of Blessington's (1789-1849) trenchant
truism, "Society punishes not the vice of its members, but
their detection." That, encapsulated, was the tragedy of Oscar
Wilde.

Over a period of twelve years or more, I was privileged to
know his son Vyvyan Holland, a quiet, kind, and gentle man.
We often used to meet and dine, frequently in Wilde's be-

loved Café Royal, that Bohemian monument of gilded and enlaureled caryatids and torquoise pillars, where deliciously we ate and imbibed and found evocative echoes of his father's age. Vyvyan revered the memory of his father whom he many times described to me as "a wonderful man." That same reverence emerges in everything Vyvyan wrote about him. But then, Wilde's son, a man of talent himself, understood the frailties of the flesh as well as recognizing the sublime color of genius.

It is not the task of this book to examine in detail the devastating fall from grace of Oscar Wilde. Others have done that with varying degrees of literacy and truth. Rather, this volume is intended to underline the genius of Wilde's masterly wit and humor, his delicious sense of high satire, ebullient fun, and, above all, his status as the supreme wit of his age. I suspect he *knew* that history would one day cast him in that role. For did he not himself proclaim, "Art is the only serious thing in the world. And the artist is the only person who is never serious"?

I hope you will find in this exposition that Oscar Wilde is seldom, if ever, serious.

Kent, England, 1979.

THE YOUNG HELLENIST

*The charm of fame is so great that we like
every object to which it is attached, even
death.*

—BLAISE PASCAL
Pensées, 1670

Before we enjoy Oscar Wilde's humor, what of his background?

His father, Sir William Wilde, was a noted ear surgeon, Surgeon-Oculist to Queen Victoria, archeologist, social lion, author of a dozen books . . . and a womanizer. Oscar's mother, Jane Francesca Elgee, daughter of a Wexford lawyer, was far from being the usual Victorian "mama." She was a writer of vitriolic verse, a celebrated contributor to *The Nation* and other Irish publications, hostess to one of Dublin's most influential salons, a fiery Protestant nationalist, and a luminous and highly accomplished feminist. Although verbose, vague, and forgetful, she was nonetheless a devoted wife and mother. Her nationalistic writings, including three controversial books, published under her nom-de-plume, "Speranza," made her name familiar to a wide readership in Ireland.

Though some Wilde biographers have evoked Jane Wilde as a figure of fun, this she was not. It must be admitted that she certainly was an eclectic eccentric; nevertheless, many sought her patronage as well as her invitations.

Despite Sir William's known string of affairs, William and Jane Wilde were devoted to each other. He accepted his wife's eccentricities with a bemused, affectionate smile; she, his lusty living with a tolerance mixed with amused understanding. To Sir William, his wife—whose lengthy period of notoriety started with a major role in the Irish revolution of 1848—was, as he once described her, "a princess of letters and a mother of rich and benevolent talent." Her involvement in the revolution all but got her incarcerated for high treason, while her *roué* husband narrowly avoided a major sex scandal in 1855.

Willie, Oscar's elder brother, destined for the law, was, like his father, to become a heavy drinker. He, too, enjoyed more than his fair share of loving ladies.

The Wilde family originally lived at 21 Westland Row, Dublin, around the corner from Merrion Square, that elegant Georgian habitat of art and artists—The Bloomsbury of Dublin—home locale of Yeats, Le Fanu, *et al.* Oscar Fingal O'Flahertie Wills Wilde, the second of three children of Sir William Wilde, was born in the house at Westland Row in 1854.

It is certain that his several pretentious Christian names were inspired by his mother's love of the bizarre and unusual. "Oscar" was chosen because it was romantically redolent of Ossian, a famed third-century Gaelic warrior-bard; it also happened conveniently to be the name of the reigning King of Sweden on whom Sir William had successfully operated to remove a cataract. In later years, Oscar was to make witty capital of his names. He explained, "My name has two O's, two F's and two W's. A name which is destined to be in everybody's mouth must not be too long. It comes so expensive in the advertisements!"

Jane's often bizarre behavior may well have had a disturbing effect on Oscar's later personality. And some have thought that his father's lechery had a strong and troublous influence on his adult development. Terence de Vere White, biographer of Oscar's parents, describes Sir William thus:

> Behind an essentially English respect for law and order and established institutions, there lay concealed in William . . . when his wants were imperious, a lack of scruple. With this went a strong streak of sentimentality. William's reputation for lechery and his wife's gigantism have provided another explanation for Oscar's homosexual tendencies.

True or false, it is virtually certain that Oscar's "elaborate vanity" was inherited from his mother. It was a sort of "pride of majesty" that played a devastating part in the misfortunes of several of the Wildes—with the single exception of Willie. But even Willie's only child, Dorothy Ierne, finished her days in Paris, dying in early middle age—a recluse, a drug addict, and a lesbian.

Throughout his life, Oscar displayed a singular devotion to his mother. He admired her tremendously, once describing her as "more talented than Elizabeth Barrett Browning." He adored her eccentric ways, which were well evident in an incident that occurred when the family had moved to No. 1 Merrion Square.

Although Sir William Wilde was a successful eye surgeon, he was also a constant victim of money troubles, such as were later often to beset Oscar. Jane had her part in this. As the money came in, she, with an endearing *folie de grandeur*, ensured its rapid disappearance through her total disregard of simple household economics. Thus, bailiffs were not infrequent visitors to the Wildes' corner house on the square. One of Jane's closest lady-friends has recorded,

> I called unexpectedly to see Jane and found the house in possession of bailiffs. There were two strange men in the hall and I heard from the weeping servant that they were "men in possession." I felt so sorry for poor Lady Wilde and hurried upstairs to the drawing-room where I knew I should find her. Jane was there indeed, but seemed not in the least troubled by the state of affairs in the house. I found her lying on the sofa reading *Prometheus Vinctus of Aeschylus* from which she began to declaim passages to me with exalted enthusiasm. She would not allow me to slip in a word of condolence, but seemed very anxious that I should share her entire admiration for the beauties of the Greek tragedian which she was reading. . . .

Daguerreotypes of Oscar the child at roughly the age of two or three show him attired in frilly, flouncy dresses looking like the embodiment of a pretty female child, with hairstyle to match. These photographs were taken when Jane was well into her third pregnancy and were, perhaps, characteristic of the manner in which middle-class Irish mothers dressed their male offspring up to the age of four or five years.

Lady Wilde longed for a daughter. Her longing was rewarded when, two years after Oscar's birth, she produced a daughter, Isola Francesca, on whom she showered a possessive affection. It is fair to say that a similar affection was lavished on her two sons, Oscar and Willie. But Jane was to be denied a full life with her daughter; Isola died at the age of ten after a week's illness. The tragedy virtually prostrated Jane for many months. Oscar, too, was deeply affected by the death of his little sister. Some years later he wrote his moving poem "Requiescat" in memory of her.

After the death of Sir William in 1876, Jane followed Oscar to London, living in much depleted circumstances on Oakley

Street, Chelsea, but bravely putting up a front of affluence and, to a degree, influence. Throughout his decade of high success, Oscar did much to support his mother. She, for her part, wrote him delightful, affectionate, gossipy letters, in one of which she revealed, "When I see you knighted, I will be happy."

At all events, in their second child Sir William and Lady Wilde produced a son who was to achieve singular academic success and social brilliance.

His first school, Portora Royal, Enniskillen, Ireland, which he attended in company with his brother, provided an inspiring introduction to academia. Oscar's infinite capacity for learning and his natural talent for the classics won for him in his last year at Portora the gold medal for the best classical scholar. The development of his classical leanings continued through and beyond the age of seventeen when he entered Trinity College, Dublin, the most distinguished university of Ireland.

This attraction to the classics, particularly to the Greek language and culture, won for him the Berkeley Gold Medal, Trinity's highest award for classics. He achieved this with his thesis on *The Fragments of the Greek Comic Poets as Edited by Meineke*. Sadly, many years later in one of his periods of near-penury, he was forced to pawn the Berkeley Medal for ready cash.

Oscar's time at Trinity and the classical education afforded him by the Reverend John Pentland Mahaffy, Professor of Ancient History (and later Proctor) at the Irish university, were highly rewarding to the scholar. There is no doubt that Reverend Mahaffy, a brilliant conversationalist ("an artist in eloquent words and vivid pauses," according to Oscar's son), was a considerable influence in the scholar's classical development. Mahaffy was later to be knighted for his academic achievements and contributions to Irish letters.

A significant event during Oscar's time at Trinity was his meeting with a fellow student, Edward "Ned" Carson—the same Ned Carson who in the years ahead, with strange irony, was destined to bring about his downfall. At Trinity, Wilde got to know Carson quite well, but they never became close friends. The two had little in common. Oscar, an outstanding Hellenist, lived for the classics. Carson, the son of an architect of Italian parentage, was destined for the bar. And while academically Oscar carried all before him, Carson on the other hand failed in his attempt for a scholarship.

It says much for Carson's integrity, however, that years later, when the eminent Charles Russell (later Sir Charles, whose law firm practices in London to this day) first attempted to brief Carson the barrister to undertake the eighth Marquis of Queensbury's legendary defense against Wilde's prosecuting action in London's High Court, Carson refused the brief, declaring that he could not bring himself "to appear against an old Trinity classmate and fellow alumnus." (That he was later persuaded to take on Queensbury's defense was brought about by revelationary evidence uncovered by Russell and his colleagues. The methods employed to obtain this evidence, although admissible in law, were declared by many at the time to be acts of "legal scavenging." But all's fair in love and law.)

Oscar's scholarship from Trinity was to win him a demyship (£95 per annum) at Magdalen College, Oxford, in October 1874, a few weeks after his twentieth birthday.

During his time at Oxford, Oscar, broad and over six feet tall, was extremely popular and "a bit of a dresser." He quickly integrated himself into university life and was heavily influenced by a handful of academic gargantuas of the day, notably Walter Pater; John Ruskin, Slade Professor of Art; and the legendary Cardinal Newman. Excited about an imminent interview in Birmingham with the erudite churchman, Wilde wrote to a friend, "I am awfully keen for this interview, not of course to argue, but merely to be in the presence of that divine man. . . ."

It was Newman, himself a brilliant wit, who was said to have met his match at a dinner at which he was placed next to the Chief Rabbi. When some succulent ham was placed before him, he turned to the Rabbi and remarked, "And to think that you mustn't eat this!" To which the Rabbi was said to have replied, "Oh, I'll undertake to eat it at Your Eminence's wedding!"

Wilde regaled his friends with the story of that same worthy cardinal who, chatting to a rather flippant undergraduate, asked him what he was going to do in life. The young man replied airily, "I'm going to take Holy Orders." Newman smiled soothingly, commenting, "Take care you get them, my son!"

It was through the influence of Newman at this period of his life that Wilde seriously considered studying for Holy Orders; that he did not do so his brother Willie ascribed to his belief that such a step would "bitterly wound" their parents. Oscar gave up the idea, but never lost his interest in the Roman church.

He became a studious, if trifle bizarre, undergraduate, advocating through his intense interest in aesthetics the principle of "Art for Art's Sake," thus echoing Pater "that the ultimate wisdom consists in expanding our lives by getting as many pulsations as possible into a given time." The scholar also expounded to all and sundry the new Age of Aestheticism based on Ruskin's theory of the "necessity of beauty, ugliness of machinery and dignity of labour"—all integral, Ruskin claimed, to "the New Age."

Wilde was not overfond of sporting activities; his Hellenistic fervor did not stretch to prowess in Athenian-type sports, nor did he like English national games. But he was able to give good account of himself in more than one college brawl. He was later to say, "I do not play cricket because it requires me to assume indecent postures!" Of the energetic game of football, he chirruped, "I feel that football is all very well as a game for rough girls, but it is hardly suitable for delicate boys!"

Wilde had a tremendous respect for Walter Pater, but he was not averse to poking a little fun at at that eminent academic. At the end of a lecture, Pater was surrounded by admiring students. He expressed the hope that they were all able to hear what he had said. "We overheard you!" quipped Oscar.

Under Professor J. P. Mahaffy's tutelage, Oscar flowered. The youthful Mahaffy, a nimble wit himself, was the academic who, when asked the difference between a man and a woman, without a second's hesitation replied, "I cannot conceive!" Under his aegis, Oscar soon became fluent in Greek. It was said that in his *viva voce* examination at Oxford Wilde had to translate from the Greek version of the New Testament. The passage, taken from one of the set books, was of the Passion. It was almost child's play to Wilde, and he translated with incredible assurance and accuracy. His examiners expressed their complete satisfaction with his effort and told him that he need not go on as was normally required. But Wilde breezily continued to translate with ease. Only after he was again told that the examiners were totally satisfied did they succeed in stopping him. Oscar looked disappointed. "Oh, do let me go on," he pleaded, "I want to see how it ends!"

On vacation, he once brought a friend back to Merrion Square, presenting his mother with this flourish: "I want to introduce you to my mother. We have founded a Society for the Suppression of Virtue!"

He left Magdalen and Oxford "covered in academic glory." During this time, he also became more and more extrovert in his mode of dress—flamboyant would be too timid a word to describe his often outrageous attire.

Before visiting the continent of Europe, he took a first class degree in Moderations and later, in 1878, gained a first class in the Honours Finals or "Greats"—a "Double First," the ambition of virtually every serious university student.

He traveled to Greece and later, in 1876, to Italy in the company of two friends, Robert Ross and Reginald Turner. He dallied with the idea of taking up a teaching post, but turned it down as "unrewarding." About this time, a fellow graduate questioned him about his future. Oscar was wittily flippant.

> God knows! I won't be an Oxford don, anyhow. Perhaps I'll be a writer, poet or dramatist. Somehow or other I'll be famous and if I'm not famous I'll be notorious! Or perhaps I'll lead the life of pleasure and rest and do nothing. . . .

To his inquirer, he musingly recalled Plato's words: "What does he say is the highest end that man can attain here below? To sit down and contemplate the good. Perhaps that will be the end of me, too!"

Wilde's success at Oxford was triumphantly sealed when news reached him that he had won the coveted Newdigate Prize, Oxford's principal prize for poetry, for his poem "Ravenna," a city he had visited on his Italian trip. It was especially rewarding that the Newdigate had earlier been won by John Ruskin during his Oxford days at Christ Church.

London beckoned the brilliant young scholar, who by this time had dubbed himself "Professor of Aesthetics." He persuaded Frank Miles, an artist and fellow student at Oxford, to share rooms with him in a street off the Strand. Sir William Wilde, who had died during Oscar's second year at Oxford, had left him a small inheritance, and soon the graduate was being discussed over influential dinner tables. His flamboyant, unconventional dress—Byronesque shirts; outsize, heavily-knotted garish neckties; braided, elegantly cut frock coats—and his penchant for surrounding himself with large, vivid, exotic sunflowers, blue orchids, green carnations, and spectacular blood-red poppies, became an animated talking-point of London society. His witty asides were constantly quoted and misquoted. He was inundated with invitations and mixed freely and easily with the leaders of society, headed by the King of the Belgians and by the Prince of Wales and his court.

So widely was Wilde discussed that *Punch* magazine, whose sphere of influence was extremely important, started to lampoon the extrovert young academic—and the extrovert young academic loved every moment of it! His popularity assumed gargantuan proportions when F. C. Burnand, the editor of *Punch*, himself penned a play entitled *The Colonel*, featuring the distinguished actor Sir Herbert Beerbohm Tree, which sizzlingly and unashamedly satirized the avant garde Oscar. Although he pretended not to recognize the likeness in the principal character of *The Colonel*, it is known that Oscar positively reveled in the notoriety. Even this accolade was soon topped by the partnership of Gilbert and Sullivan, who characterized the young poet with biting derision in their new operetta, *Patience*. Publicity may not be good for the soul, but it certainly aids the ego.

Rather than cutting him down to size, the overall effect of these and other satirical onslaughts sent Wilde's popular image spiralling to heady heights.

The greater his social acclaim, the more he was satirized, and the more he dressed the part—outrageously! He wrote sonnets to Henry Irving, Sarah Bernhardt, Ellen Terry, and others. He was an elitist with a touch of the showman, who appeared to rise above all criticism. He briefly dismissed his critics with "Caricature is the tribute mediocrity pays to genius!"

His wit was not only widely quoted but copied even on the stage of the music halls, then a favorite entertainment medium of the masses.

It was Wilde who was the progenitor of Millais's celebrated painting of Lily Langtry in her famous black dress. "The trouble is," Millais told Wilde, "she looks beautiful for fifty-five minutes in every hour; for five she is quite amazing!" Millais could certainly recognize and appreciate real beauty, for had he not married the exquisite Euphemia ("Effie"), former wife of John Ruskin who, legend had it, on his wedding night to Effie got cold feet and did not consummate his marriage to that erstwhile lady? Millais did rather better.

Wilde was a flamboyant star at the private viewing at the Royal Academy when Millais's painting of Lily Langtry was unveiled. The picture caused a sensation, and the area had to be roped off to hold pack the pressing crowds. Wilde led the acclaim, surrounded by his new-found acolytes. He reveled in his association with the notorious Lily and quickly became the male cynosure of her influential circle of sycophants.

Ever generous to his friends, Frank Miles—who described himself as "an artist who specialized in painting beautiful women"—sketched and painted Lily Langtry on Oscar's introduction.

Lily married a penniless dullard, Edward Langtry. Procured by Lord Suffield, she was to become the mistress of Bertie, the Prince of Wales who became King Edward VII. Like many influential men in London, Oscar, too, fell "violently in love" with Lily, displaying such extrovert admiration as one night to sleep on her doorstep. Whistler, the artist and wit, similarly became her slave. "She is perfect. Her beauty is exquisite, her manners more exquisite still." Lord Leighton, too, painted her; Gladstone was devoted to her and Wilde, quite simply, adored her.

Or did he? Certainly he wrote and published a poem in her

honor which he inscribed, "To Helene, formerly of Troy, but now of London." When she turned to acting, he wrote *Lady Windermere's Fan* expressly for her.

Inevitably, Oscar, the brilliant newcomer, attracted the interest of leading artistic minds of the day, among them Aubrey Beardsley, Sir William Rothenstein, Max Beerbohm, Bernard Shaw, and the unavoidable Frank Harris, who moved—omnipresent, tireless, and talkative—on the periphery of the influential art and social circles of the time, largely through his work as a journalist and author.

Gilbert and Sullivan's operetta *Patience* settled down to enjoy a marked success at London's Savoy Theatre, gaily lampooning the Oscar Wilde character who "walked down Piccadilly with a poppy or a lily in [his] medieval hand":

> Then a sentimental passion
> of a vegetable fashion
> must excite your languid spleen,
> An attachment à la Plato
> for a bashful young potato,
> or a not-too-French French bean!
> Though the Philistines may jostle,
> you will rank as an apostle
> in the high aesthetic band,
> If you walk down Piccadilly
> with a poppy or a lily
> in your mediaeval hand.
> And everyone will say,
> As you walk your flowery way,
> "If he's content with a vegetable love
> which would certainly not suit me,
> Why, what a most particularly pure
> young man this pure young man must be!"

"To the pure all things are impure" might have been acidulous Oscar's comment to this pointed lampoon. Instead, his amused reaction was, "Anyone could have walked down Piccadilly like that! The difficult thing to achieve was to make people believe that I had done it!"

His fame spread rapidly to the Continent. A published collection of his poems gained him further widespread comment. He loomed larger than life, saturated in social success, a lionized Leviathan.

The producers of *Patience* hit on the idea of staging the show in America. Oscar was simultaneously invited to undertake a year's lecture tour of the States—a shrewd publicity move on the part of the play's promoters. His lecture theme? *The Principles of Aestheticism.*

The year was 1882. The Wildean wit was ready to explode in the New World.

AMERICA! AMERICA!

Wit makes its own welcome and levels all distinctions
—Ralph Waldo Emerson
& "The Comic," *Letters & Social Aims*, 1876

Before leaving for America, Wilde, with Frank Miles, left the rooms in Salisbury Street, Strand, for more modest accommodation at No. 3 Tite Street, Chelsea—a few hundred yards from No. 16 where he was later to live when married.

Although acclaimed in London literary circles, he was not as yet making a fortune; indeed, he was pretty close to penury but believed this could be remedied by his American lecture tour.

Determined to write for the theater, he started work on his first play, *Vera, or The Nihilists*—at the time topical subject material, based as it was on the cult of Nihilism then sweeping Tsarist Russia. He worked studiously, creating clever lines in a play that glowed with wit: "Life is much too important a thing ever to talk seriously about it." Arguing that "Nothing is impossible in Russia but reform," the play considered that "Men of thought should have nothing to do with action," and, with sly Wildean iconoclasm, "He would stab his best friend for the sake of writing an epigram on his tombstone." And what of Russia's rampant communism? "What a Communist he is! He would have an equal distribution of sin as well as property!"

His dialogue included this biting epicurean sally: "To make a good salad is to be a brilliant diplomatist—the problem is entirely the same in both cases: to know exactly how much oil one must put with one's vinegar!" He extended the epicurean analogy with "A cook and a diplomatist! An excellent parallel! If I had a son who was a fool I'd make him one or the other," and a later remark was certainly calculated to win him applause in Tsarist Russia: "There is always more brass than brains in an aristocracy!" He enunciated that "Good kings are the only dangerous enemies that modern democracy has," and Russians might well have admired the smooth texture of this thought: "I have no ambition to be a popular hero, to be crowned with laurels one year and be pelted with stones the next; I prefer dying peaceably in my own bed."

His character, The President of the Nihilists, quipped "We speak the truth to one another here. . . ." Prince Paul, the Tzar's chief minister, replied, "How misleading you must find it!"

In this final shaft from *Vera, or The Nihilists*, he pushed home that "The typical spendthrift is always giving away what he needs most."

With the play finished, and America looming ahead, Oscar Wilde was disappointed to find considerable resistance to it. He did in fact receive an offer from a leading actress-impresario, Mrs. Bernard Beere, but the deal was canceled because of the uneasy political climate caused by the assassination of Tsar Alexander II. After all, the British Prince of Wales was related to the assassinated Tsar's widow....

On 2 January 1882, Oscar Wilde arrived in New York to undertake his lecture tour, a tour that was to last just short of a year. He was booked to address assemblies of college students, "Green Book" matrons, literary societies, workers' clubs, educationalists—and metal miners!

On his arrival in New York, reporters who mobbed him on the boat were disappointed by his appearance, said to be "more like that of an athlete than an aesthete." True, he wore his characteristic long hair and a bottle-green, fur-lined overcoat and sported a round sealskin cap on his head. Incongruously, he was a giant in stature, and his fists looked like a prize fighter's. Expecting the press to question him about aesthetics, he was instead questioned as to how he liked his eggs fried; what was his favorite night attire; how he trimmed his fingernails; and at what temperature he liked his bath water!

His answers displayed disdain with the inane questions. Disappointed, the reporters buttonholed his fellow passengers for "overheard" quotes of a livelier nature. Rising eagerly to the bait, they had heard Wilde complain that the trip had been tame, "deucedly stupid," that the roaring ocean did not roar, and that nothing less than a storm that swept the ship's bridge would have given him real pleasure! That was enough for the reporters, who told their readers that Wilde "was disappointed with the Atlantic Ocean . . . !" a phrase that got him far more publicity than his views on aestheticism or even a sparkling riposte on the theme of fried eggs!

Wilde realized he had done his reputation less than justice; but his buffoonery was to soar the moment he stepped ashore. "Have you anything to declare?" asked a customs official. "I have nothing to declare except my genius!" he quipped. That was as telling a remark as any visitor to America had ever made, and it echoed 'round the continent. He was getting into his stride, amusingly observing that "Life in America is one long expectoration!"

He was quick to make it perfectly plain to his host country that he deeply deplored the American lack of manners. And he was not to change his opinion, even if his reticence to withdraw did provoke further publicity. Anyway, he regarded "scandal as gossip made tedious by morality," and he peremptorily silenced his American college audiences with: "In America, the young are always ready to give to those who are older than themselves the full benefit of their inexperience."

Wilde lectured exhaustively and exhaustingly in over seventy American towns, starting at the Chickering Hall, New York. When on occasion his perorations on aesthetics met with tepid enthusiasm, he found himself in clashes with an openly hostile press. Even in the tougher areas of the Far West, where he was sometimes openly ridiculed by audiences and dubbed "The Ass-Thete," Wilde never lost his refined, acerbic sense of humor. He took raucousness in good part, firing right back with his wit. And his amazing capacity for alcohol became legendary—he could, and did, drink hardened miners and cowboys under the table.

The fact that he was positively lionized by American women did not tend to make him over-popular with American men! But he was more than equal to the barbs and insults that came his way. "When good Americans die, they go to Paris: when bad Americans die, they stay in America," he smiled. And, "Of course, if one had enough money to go to America, one would not go!"

Well aware of the provocative publicity he was creating, he quickly let those of the new continent know that his importance was such that he had to hire not one but two secretaries to cope with his tour. "One for my autographs and one for requested locks of my hair!" he explained.

America was duly impressed, but there was more to come. ". . . within six weeks of arriving here," he drawled, "one of the secretaries had died of writer's cramp and the other was completely bald!" His audiences roared their approval.

He continued lightheartedly to indulge his penchant for baiting Yankees, as when he met the taciturn Richard Harding Davis. "So you are from Philadelphia where Washington is buried?" said Oscar. "Nonsense! He's buried in Mount Vernon," Davis replied tartly. Wilde, not a whit disconcerted at Davis's rude manner, switched the talk to a new French painter. "Do let's hear what Mr. Davis thinks of him," he purred to his listeners. "Americans always talk so amusingly of art." Davis snapped back, "I never talk about things when I don't know the facts!" Wilde flashed, "That, my dear fellow, must limit your conversation frightfully!" Had Wilde not already declared, "Arguments are to be avoided; they are always vulgar and often convincing!"?

But he did not always have his own way in America. The city of Boston is credited with having remonstrated in kind at the "superciliousness" of Oscar Wilde. "You're Philistines," Wilde accused his Boston audience, "who have bogusly invaded the sacred sanctum of Art!" A voice in the audience retorted, "And you're driving us forth with the jawbone of an ass!"

While assuring America that most people "die of creeping common sense," he dressed himself in cowboy outfits and Stetson hats, firing droll verbal volleys in state after state. He was taking America by storm. The customers had never seen or heard anything quite like him.

Cavorting in the sinisterly named town of Leadville,

Colorado, Wilde came up with what has now become an "immortal" satirical saying. Like most saloons out West, Leadville's was noted for an unending supply of honky-tonk piano music. There appeared at the time to be a relatively high mortality rate among the Leadville saloon pianoforte exponents and, as someone succinctly observed, this was due either to a high standard of musical appreciation among the drinkers or an abysmally low standard of musicianship among the pianists. It was duly confirmed when Wilde looked up above the piano, and chuckled when he read the notice pinned there: "Don't shoot the pianist—he's doing his best!"

At this stage of his tour, he roundly declared to the amusement of many that "The discovery of America was the beginning of the death of Art," and went on to qualify this with "Perhaps after all America has never been discovered? I myself would merely say that it has been detected!" This was the stuff they wanted, and this was precisely the stuff that Wilde gave them during the grueling months of his whistle-stop tour.

Questioned on the subject of hate, he quipped, "Always forgive your enemies; nothing annoys them so much!" And on life and living, he observed, "The soul is born old but grows young. That is the comedy of life. The body is born young and grows old. That's life's tragedy."

He was later astringently to repeat in *The Picture of Dorian Gray*, that "American girls are as clever at concealing their parents as English women are at concealing their past!"

And he wasn't going to leave Leadville without giving them something else to remember him by: "I looked at all the shining silver I saw coming from the mines," he said, "knowing that it would be made into ugly dollars. It made me so sad!"

His ostentatious dress provoked the American press into

inquiring why, in the relatively warm winter of 1882, he perpetually carried his heavy fur coat with him. Wilde replied, "I carry it to hide the hideous sofas in your hotel rooms!"

And he could not forbear observing, when comparing the American penal system with the English, that "The Americans are great hero-worshippers. They always take their heroes from the criminal classes!"

It seemed that American women, on balance, passed muster. He remarked, "American women on the whole are quite charming, but American men—alas!" which endeared him still less to American males.

But the more he provoked, the more publicity he received, and the more lecture invitations poured in. One day, on receiving a cable from a town called Griggsville beseeching him to "Lecture us on Aesthetics," he took one look at the cable and hastily penned the reply, "Begin by changing the name of your town!"

He deplored America's "ignorance of the Arts," which he illustrated by declaring,

> . . . so infinitesimal did I find the knowledge of Art, west of the Rocky Mountains, that an art patron (one who in his day had been a miner) actually sued the railroad company for damages on the plea that the plaster-cast Venus de Milo which he had imported from Paris had been delivered minus the arms! What is more surprising still is that he won his case with full damages!

And he further accused, "Art in America has no marvel, beauty no meaning, and the past no message."

In conversation, he caused a squirm or two with this sally: "Some Southern Americans have a melancholy tendency to date every event of importance by the late war. 'How beautiful the moon is tonight.' I once remarked to a gentleman standing near me. 'Yes,' was his reply, 'but you should have seen it before the war!' "

The mining towns seemed to fascinate Wilde. While in Denver, on his way to Leadville, the city where it was alleged "men are men and those who aren't are dead meat," he was warned that Leadville might live up to its name as far as he and his traveling impresario were concerned. His disarming reply was, "Nothing they could do to my travelling manager would intimidate me!"

He was invited to open a new mine vein with a silver drill, the lode having been christened "The Oscar" in his honor. Commented Wilde, "I had hoped that in their grand simple way they would have offered me shares in 'The Oscar,' but in their artless, untutored fashion they did not mention such a reward!"

Wilde romped from success to success, seldom out of the newspapers. He touched nerve after nerve. *Sell yourself—and sell yourself hard* was the American precept of success. Oscar took it to heart and capitalized on it. He was, unquestionably, a unique import; it was even arranged for a firm of music publishers, W. A. Evans & Bros. of Bromfield Street, Boston, Mass., to publish a "musical diversion" in his honor. It was called *The Oscar Wilde Gallop*, arranged by "a gentleman named Snow."

Americans laughed uproariously when Oscar, seeing the Mississippi in full, raging flood, turned to his hosts and observed, "No well-behaved river should act that way!" And across in Cincinnati, he cryptically informed newspapermen, "I'm amazed your criminals don't plead the frightful ugliness of your city as an excuse for their crimes!"

His clipped, droll comments were echoed in banner headlines. And he kept up the pace with gusto. "America reminds me of one of Edgar Allan Poe's exquisite poems—it is full of belles!" While playing poker on the "lecture train," he suggested the game was "Like most of the distinctly national products of America, it seems to have been imported from abroad!"

He held forth on America's vastness and its communications:

> It is only fair to admit that the American can and does exaggerate; but even his exaggeration has a rational belief. It is not founded on wit or fancy; it does not spring from any poetic imagination: it is simply an earnest attempt on the part of the language to keep pace with the enormous size of the country. It is evident that where it takes one twenty-four hours to go across a single parish, and seven days steady railroad travelling to keep a dinner engagement in another State, the ordinary resources of human speech are quite inadequate to the strain put on them, and new linguistic forms have to be invented, new methods of description resorted to. . . . But this is nothing more than the fatal influence of geography upon adjectives; for naturally humorous the American male certainly is not!

Some years later he was to sum up, albeit tongue-in-cheek, his overall impressions of America. He did this in the essay "The Decay of Lying" in his book *Intentions*.

> . . . the crude commercialism of America, its materialist spirit, its indifference to the poetical side of things, and its lack of imagination and of high unattainable ideals, are entirely due to that country having adopted for its national hero a man who, according to his own confession, was incapable of telling a lie.

> . . . It is not too much to say that the story of George Washington and the cherry tree has done more harm, and in a shorter space of time, than any other moral tale in the whole of literature—and the amusing part of the whole thing is that the story of the cherry tree is an absolute myth!

Despite his phenomenally successful tour, Oscar returned to London and his old haunts somewhat more sober in dress and with surprisingly little ready cash in his pocket. You could not in those days debit the tax man with "expenses." Additionally, Oscar knew how to spend money and had done so. But he had also broadened his circle widely by meeting, and in most cases making friends of, many influential Americans, notably Walt Whitman, General Grant, Henry Ward Beecher, Louisa May Alcott, Jefferson Davis, Oliver Wendell Holmes, and Henry Wadsworth Longfellow.

OTHER PLACES, OTHER THINGS

The wit we wish we had spoils the wit we have

—JEAN BAPTISTE LOUIS GRESSETT, *Le Méchant*, 1745

Wilde's acidulous comments were not confined to America and Americans. He could be—and frequently was—astringent in his observations on other countries and cultures, as well as characteristically amusing when giving his view on man, the animal: "I sometimes think that God in creating man somewhat overestimated His ability"

He could even be waspish about that heroic band of brothers and sisters within the confines of established religion. "Missionaries are the divinely provided food for destitute and underfed cannibals. Whenever they are on the brink of starvation, Heaven in its infinite mercy, sends them a nice plump missionary!"

And, Irish to the marrow, he wasn't over-generous to those who provided the principal platform for his fame—England

and the English. In "The English Renaissance of Art" he referred to "those things in which the English public never forgives—youth, power, and enthusiasm," and later observed that the English "think that a cheque can solve every problem in life." In "The Critic as an Artist," he took the view that "The English public always feels perfectly at ease when a mediocrity is talking to it."

Wilde, inordinately proud of his Irish ancestry, was impishly aware of the Irishman's penchant for verbosity. "Teach the English how to talk and the Irish how to listen; then society will be quite civilised." And who could quarrel with his assertion, "Experience is the name which everyone gives to his mistakes?"

He loved to bait the English. "The English have really everything in common with the Americans except, of course, language." And his mordant summary of his later English-Scottish tour underlines this. "I need hardly say that we were delighted and amused at the typical English way in which our ideas were misunderstood. They took our epigrams as earnest, and our parodies as prose!" And hear the Titan of letters in the *Saturday Review* of 17 November 1894: "The English are always degrading the truth into facts. When a truth becomes a fact, it loses all its intellectual value."

In 1895, R. Golding Bright,° then a newspaperman (he afterwards became a leading theatrical manager and agent) had a habit of writing to literary celebrities of the day firmly and uncompromisingly taking uninvited leave to criticize their work. It was in such a vein that Bright wrote to Wilde. Oscar replied the same day. "Sir, I have read your letter. I see that to the brazen everything is brass!"

Wilde had an innate love of France and the French, but he was seldom backward in keeping them in his sights on the

---

° Shaw's book, *Advice to a Young Critic*, is a documentary record of Bright's letters to him.

firing line. After Ireland and England, he regarded France as his third home but first love. "The great superiority of France over England is that in France every bourgeois wants to be an artist, whereas in England every artist wants to be a bourgeois." And not without some truth did he observe, "In Paris, one can lose one's time most delightfully; but one can never lose one's way!"

Truth to tell, he certainly seemed unenchanted with Scotland and the Road to the Isles. "For a man to be both a genius and a Scotsman is the very stage for tragedy. Your Scotsman believes only in success. . . . God saved the genius of Robert Burns to poetry by driving him through drink to failure. . . ." Of the deeper reaches of tartaned art and artistry, he had this to say: "To fail and to die young is the only hope for a Scotsman who wishes to remain an artist."

There were times when he took a pretty dim view of London and certain of its districts, for instance: "Bayswater is a place where people always get lost and where there are no guides," and West Kensington was not his favourite place, either: "West Kensington is a district to which you drive until the horse drops dead, when the cabman gets down to make enquiries . . ."

He took, too, a dim view of Russia and the Russians, although he was to publish a highly controversial and somewhat surprizing essay, "The Soul of Man Under Socialism," in which he opined, "A Russian who lives happily under the present system of government in Russia must either believe that man has no soul or that, if he has, it is not worth developing."

Wilde never went to Australia, but that didn't stop him from commenting, "When I look at the map and see what an ugly country Australia is, I feel that I want to go there and see if it cannot be changed into a more beautiful form."

He might have been accused of anti-Semitism with his

published description of the Jewish moneylending fraternity of his time as "gentlemen who breathe through their noses and make you pay through yours," but it was a remark inspired by his all-pervading sense of fun. He later clamped down on an outburst of Victorian ire towards the Jewish race with "Such hostility is vulgar and ungrateful; they are the only people who lend money. . . ."

Wilde would speed off to Paris whenever funds permitted. On one such visit, when his fame had spread throughout France, he had dinner with André Gide who, a little the worse for wine, took it upon himself to criticize one of Oscar's plays—the one-act *Salomé*. Wilde listened attentively to Gide's lucid critique. Gide finally stopped and stared aggressively at Oscar, fully expecting a resentful outburst. Instead, he heard Wilde quietly observe, "André, I put all my genius into my life; I only put my talent into my writings!"

There was, too, the memorable occasion in Paris when Wilde was introduced to a woman who, doubtless as a result of some sort of neurosis, seemed to take an infinite pride in her abject ugliness. "Don't you think," she asked Oscar, "that I am the ugliest woman in all Paris?" "No, madame," replied Oscar, "not in Paris alone—in all the world!"

Wilde doubtless believed his own aphorism that "Artists, like Gods, must never leave their pedestals," except perhaps to deal with their own publicity, for let it be acknowledged that Wilde was scarcely unaware of the press value of his celebrity status.

Frank Harris, who was known to be envious of Wilde, recalls in one of his books *(Bernard Shaw,* Gollancz, 1931) a salutary lesson provided by Oscar in terms of self-projection:

I remember Oscar Wilde bringing me one day, in the early 'eighties, I think, a cutting from "The Westminister Gazette" in which we were both mentioned, and rather contemptuously.

"Have you seen it, Frank?" "Yes, I have seen it." "What have you written about it?" "Nothing. I am not going to write about such nonsense." "Oh, Frank, you are quite wrong. They give you a column to write about yourself, and what's more, they pay you too. You ought never to neglect such opportunities. That is the way to make yourself known." "I do not agree with you," I said, "and I am not going to bother about it." But I soon found that Oscar's determination to write about himself whenever he got the opportunity was the successful line to adopt, at any rate in a democracy. . . .

Harris, whose main claim to fame in the twentieth century is as a seducer and pornographer and the author of *My Life and Loves,* which was banned in England until the permissive age of the 'sixties, was rude, robust, and conceitedly extrovert; W. L. George summed him up pointedly with "One does not meet Frank Harris—one collides with him!" Harris was a declared cynic and could be offensive to the point of insult, as Bosie Douglas would have agreed. Douglas once greeted him scornfully in the Café Royal with "Ah, Ancient Pistol!" "Well roared, Bottom!" cried Harris.

Harris and others have recorded the view that Bernard Shaw did not like Wilde and that Wilde was not overfond of Shaw, and the facts seem to bear this out. There were those who believed that Shaw was jealous of Wilde.

When Shaw, as a young man, emerged from his native Ireland and moved to England, he began writing a column for a London weekly publication. At this time Oscar Wilde was enjoying his spiraling vogue as a wit and epigrammatist. One evening an acquaintance, calling on Wilde, picked up a copy of the paper to which Shaw was contributing. Scanning Shaw's provocative article, signed with the author's initials, he said to his host, "I say, Wilde, who is this chap GBS who's doing a department for this sheet?" "He's a young Irishman named Shaw," said Wilde. "Rather forceful isn't he?" "Forceful," echoed the other. "Well, rather!" "My word, how he does cut and slash! He doesn't seem to spare anyone he knows. I should say he is in a fair way to make himself a lot of enemies." "Well," said Wilde, "as yet he hasn't become prominent enough to have any enemies. But none of his friends like him. . . ."

It must be said, however, that Shaw was usually kind to Wilde in his critiques of Oscar's plays and other writings. There was often badinage between the two, and a delightful story concerns the already well-established Wilde and the youthful Shaw who was himself fast becoming a literary "name."

The two met in the rooms of Fitzgerald Malloy in Red Lion Square, Bloomsbury, and it is apparent that on this occasion Oscar had decided to be a good listener. Shaw, delighted at receiving Wilde's unqualified attention, took the opportunity to let himself go on the subject of a magazine he was planning. He talked uninterruptedly for over half an hour, describing in detail the proposed format, the contributors he planned to seek, the outlook, policy, scope, and general potential of the project.

When Shaw finally came to a halt, Wilde, with much charm and understanding, observed quietly, "Most interesting, Mr. Shaw! Most interesting! But you have forgotten something. You haven't told us the title of your proposed magazine." "Oh, as for that," said Shaw, "I'd want to impress my own personality on the public. It would be called 'Shaw's Magazine.' " He banged the table with his fist. "Shaw! Shaw! Shaw!" he added loudly. "Yes," smiled Oscar, "and how would you spell it?"

Could it have been this meeting that later was to provide Wilde with one of his most incisive aphorisms, "Everything happens to everybody sooner or later if there is time enough"?

Frank Harris is said to have been regarded by Wilde as a

friend. It is true that he helped Wilde by featuring his writings in *The Fortnightly Review* and other literary outlets with which he was concerned either as editor or adviser. The other side of the coin was that he shrewdly recognized Wilde's genius early, and Wilde repaid his interest by showing him loyalty and extreme generosity.

It is also true that Harris tried to prevent Wilde from bringing about his own downfall and, creditably, did not desert the artist and poet in his hour of extreme travail. He was also one of the first to capitalize on Wilde's notoriety and fame at the end of Oscar's life by speedily writing his biography.

Harris's biography of Shaw—which contained a diffident postscript by GBS—gossips about Wilde's relationship with Shaw and about his own activities when Oscar's tragic downfall struck; it has echoes of Voltaire's "My enemies I know, God save me from my friends." Here, again, is Harris on Wilde and Shaw:

> Oscar was present once when Shaw delivered an address on Socialism. Robert Ross pleased Shaw by telling him that Shaw's address had inspired Oscar to write "The Soul of Man Under Socialism. . . ."

> Shaw does remember a pleasant meeting with Wilde, when both dropped their guard. It was at an exhibition in Chelsea, which was so unsophisticated that the mere idea of their both being at it amused them enormously. This was Shaw's first experience of Oscar as a story-teller. Shaw had not to talk, but simply to listen to a raconteur. Wilde was dressed, like Shaw, in tweeds instead of a frock coat. They got on splendidly. . . .

> The only other meeting Shaw remembers was at the Café Royal, when Wilde's liberty was in danger; in fact, on the eve of his case against the Marquis of Queensbury. I was urging Wilde to skip to France, as he had not a chance of winning his suit. This meeting was embarrassing because Shaw, who had

praised Wilde's first plays, had criticized "The Importance of Being Earnest," as a really heartless play. . . .

When Wilde was sent to prison, Shaw drafted a petition for his release. On meeting Willie Wilde, Oscar's brother, a journalist, at a theatre in St. Martin's Lane, Shaw spoke to him about the petition, Shaw said that nobody would sign it except himself and Stewart Headlam, and that as they were both notorious *frondeurs* their signatures would do more harm than good. Willie assented. So the petition fell to the ground; and what became of Shaw's draft Shaw himself doesn't know. . . .

When Wilde had done more than half of his inhuman sentence, he was reported to be in bad health, and I busied myself to get him released before his time. The head of the Prison's Commission, Sir Evelyn Ruggles-Brise, told me that if a dozen literary men of distinction would sign the petition for Wilde's release on the ground that the sentence of two year's hard labour had been condemned by a Royal Commission as too severe, he had no doubt that the Home Secretary would advise the Queen to remit the rest of Wilde's sentence. I have told in "The Life and Confessions of Oscar Wilde" how I tried to get Meredith to sign the Petition and failed. After various other failures I asked Shaw; he shook his head and said, Oh, I'm not the right person; get respectable signatures.

Still later, when Wilde after his imprisonment lived as an exile in Paris, Shaw made it a point to send him inscribed copies of all his books as they came out. Wilde did the same to him. The real thing they had in common was that they both were considered as court jesters and they both resented it. Thus they treated each other as distinguished and important personalities.

Now and then they touched a common chord, as in the case when they agreed they were both more than witty triflers in words. When the Chicago anarchists were sentenced to death (I wrote a novel, "The Bomb," about them afterwards), Shaw tried to get up a petition for the release of the imprisoned men. Of all the courageous rebels (in parlours) he got only one signa-

ture. That was Oscar Wilde's. It won Wilde Shaw's consideration for the rest of Wilde's life.

William Morris, when he was slowly dying, said he enjoyed a
visit from Wilde more than from anybody else, and Shaw tells
me that he can understand me when I write that I would
rather have Wilde back than any other friend I ever talked to.
And at this point, Shaw makes an excellent analysis of Wilde,
declaring that Oscar was "incapable of friendship, though not
of the most touching kindness, on occasion."

He records a gaffe made by Willie Wilde. In defending Oscar
to Shaw after Oscar's imprisonment, Willie remarked with
maladroit pathos—"Oscar was *not* a man of bad character. You
could have trusted him with a woman anywhere. . . ."

"The first thing," Shaw once wrote to me about Oscar, "we ask
a servant for is a testimonial to honesty, sobriety and industry,
for we soon find out that they are the scarce things and that
geniuses are as common as rats." I pointed out to Shaw that
this was the English shoddy in him. Genius is the rarest thing
on earth, whereas nine human beings out of ten have honesty,
sobriety and industry beaten into them by life. "If so," he replied, the crafty expert that he is in repartee, "it is the tenth
that comes my way."

But Shaw had little real sympathy for Wilde; did he not write
of him as "ending his life as an unproductive drunkard and
swindler"? How he hates drinkers!

Invitations continued to flood into Wilde's room; the once-
gauche Lily Langtry frequently received Oscar at her home—
much to the chagrin of her husband Edward, who was accepted in society solely by reason of the astonishing social
success of his wife. It was at the Langtry's that Oscar first met
the mercurial socialite Moreton Frewen, who had married the

fair-haired Clara, one of the three "fabulous Jerome girls." Cambridge-educated and known to his friends jocularly as "mortal Ruin," he had largely disposed of nearly £20,000—a fortune in those days—on hunting by day, gambling in country houses in the evening, while exploring the bedroom corridors by night for Lily Langtry and other beautiful prey. Knowing everyone in society, from kings to "paupers" like himself, he discovered Rudyard Kipling, bought worthless gold mines with other people's money, and finally joined his uncle Winston Churchill in the House of Commons as member of Parliament for West Cork, Ireland.

Frewen liked Oscar except insofar as he accurately considered the writer and poet a rival for Lily Langtry's affections. One evening Lily invited Frewen to join her dinner party, which included Wilde and Ouida ((Maria de la Ramee (1839-1908)), whose pen name was "Ouida"), the famed novelist. This presented a joyful prospect to Wilde, who adored baiting Ouida; the occasion was to prove no exception. "Have you ever considered, my dear Ouida, what your books stand for?" Oscar flippantly questioned the authoress. "Pray, do tell me what is their keynote; their motivation?" Ouida, with characteristic grandeur of gesture and phrase, slammed into the poet, "Their motivation, Oscar—their keynote as you call it—is a vehement protest against the absurdity of the outmoded institution of marriage," said this nineteenth-century precursor of Women's Lib. "One should base marriage on firm principles of careful selection, affinity and, lastly, sex," she added with aggressive verve. "But surely," purred Oscar, "girls choose husbands because they do, in your words, select them." "You are speaking of dullard dukes and other titled inebriates," snapped Ouida, impressively letting drop the names of three ducal worthies.

"These types," she persisted, "demand fidelity in order to

hand on vast estates and treasures to their sons. There is precious little beauty in your aristocracy—but then beauty is such a rare commodity today. Given free selection, it should be universal."

"But what of the men?" interposed Frewen. "May they not also select for themselves? And what happens to the home if everyone is out in the marriage market doing the selecting. . . . ?"

Ouida snorted like a war-horse and plowed grimly on. "Men," she snapped, "fools that they are, spend most of their working and leisure time examining the household books when they should be devoting their energies to the interests of the State. . . ." "Looking for even prettier women?" ventured Wilde, with a gentle smile. The party, except for Ouida, broke up in laughter.

Moreton Frewen, while not within the close Wilde coterie, kept up a tenuous friendship with Oscar over several years. They met on various occasions in London and New York, notably when Wilde was given an elegant dinner party by W. D. Duncan at No. 1 Fifth Avenue, where Duncan, Frewen, William Travers, (the distinguished American lawyer), and others were regaled by Wilde with tortuously funny stories of the aesthete's American lecture tour.

It was in New York, too, that Frewen, used the presence of Wilde and Lily Langtry to repay in part his millionaire father-in-law, Leonard Jerome, for his hospitality with "introductions to amuse Leonard"—so described by him. This was just prior to Lily's American acting debut in Cheyenne in W. S. Gilbert's *Pygmalion and Galatea*. Frewen had also been on the quayside to welcome Oscar to America at the start of his celebrated lecture tour. If Moreton Frewen had won Lily Langtry physically, as it is believed he did, it was Wilde who won her heart; they remained close friends for many years.

When troubles beset him, she was the first to offer him a substantial cash sum to finance his escape from England to France. Oscar, much moved by the gesture, refused the offer with a warm kiss and an emotional hug.

ON COOKS AND COQUELIN

Wit's an unruly engine, wildly striking some-
times a friend, sometimes the engineer
                            —George Herbert
                            (The Church Porch)
                            The Temple, 1633

If Wilde's treatment of R. Golding Bright, the theatrical agent-cum-journalist referred to earlier, had been dismissive, he was no less so on the subject of English writers and writing: "No modern literary work of any worth has been produced in English by an English writer—except, of course, Bradshaw.° "

There's an element of truth applicable today in these words written by Wilde not far short of a hundred years ago: "If in the last century England tried to govern Ireland with an insolence that was intensified by race hatred and religious prejudice, she has sought to rule her in this century with a stupidity that is aggravated by good intentions. . . ." He regarded what was known as "sound English common-sense" as ". . . the

---

° Author of a railway guide

inherited stupidity of the race." And what or who had so displeased him to inspire this "scurrilous" aphorism: "The English have a miraculous power of turning wine into water"?

The culinary ladies below stairs in Victorian times weren't too popular with him, either. "The British cook," he observed, "is a foolish woman who should be turned for her indignities into a pillar of salt which she never knows how to use!"

Although elsewhere in this book Oscar holds forth with witty bitchiness on the female of the species in general, he took a privileged view of a certain clique. "There are only five women in London worth talking to and two of these can't be admitted into decent society!"

He could, as much as on England, be very provocative on the subject of his adopted capital city. "Flowers are as common in the country," he said, "as people are in London!" And the color content of the London scene left him pretty jaded, too.

> . . . Wearied of the houses, you turn to contemplate the street itself; you have nothing to look at but chimneypot hats, men with sandwich boards, vermillion letter boxes, and [you] do that even at the risk of being run over by an emerald-green omnibus. . . .

During a talk with him, the eminent South African writer Olive Schreiner explained to Wilde that she lived in the unfashionable East End of London because "there the people don't wear masks." Quipped Wilde, "And I live in the West End of London because they do!"

Overhearing somebody in the street observe of him, "There goes that bloody fool, Oscar Wilde," the writer turned to his companion and commented, "It's extraordinary how soon one gets known in London!"

Not only London, but Britain as we know her often evoked disparaging comment from Oscar. He is on record as declaring, "To disagree with three fourths of the British public on all points is one of the first elements of sanity, one of the deepest consolations in all moments of spiritual doubt. . . ."

For all his cryptic comments at the expense of the English and their capital city, he could always do a volte-face and fire in the opposite direction with deadly accuracy.

"Town life," he quipped, "nourishes and perfects all the more civilized elements in man. Shakespeare wrote nothing but doggerel lampoon before he came to London and never penned a line after he left."

On one occasion before an assembled group, Frank Harris who was addicted to plagiarism in conversation told as his own an anecdote that everyone recognized as a paraphrase of a story by Anatole France. A silence followed, broken whimsically by Wilde. "Frank," he said gravely, "Anatole France would have spoiled that story!"

When actress Mary Anderson rejected his commissioned play, *The Duchess of Padua*, Oscar, in mock self-deprecation, "bemoaned" to Robert Sherard, "Pity, my dear Robert, we shan't be dining with the Duchess tonight!"

Although rarely performed as a play, some of Wilde's lines in *The Duchess of Padua*, written in blank verse, have taken on a patina of immortality:

A sermon is a sorry sauce when you have nothing to eat it with.

DUKE: Have prudence with your dealings with the world. Be not too hasty; act on the second thought, first impulses are generally good. . . .

and, from the same play, philosophically,

We are each our own devil, and we make this world our hell.

Softly, too,

They do not sin at all who sin for love.

When in later years Wilde was questioned by a newspaper reporter about the cool reception of *The Duchess of Padua*, he averred, "the play in itself was a great success. But the audience was a profound failure!" It was, in fact, his least successful play, but the remark was Oscar laughing at himself again.

His stay in Paris surprisingly did not provide him with a renewed zest for work. While there he penned only "The Harlot's House," later published in *The Dramatic Review*, but his popularity with the Parisian Bohemians rose steadily. He dined and drank with Mallarmé, Victor Hugo, Daudet, Pissarro, Verlaine, Edgar Degas, and Emile Zola. Zola appeared perplexed and peeved by Oscar's extrovert wit and personality. At a formal dinner Zola was called on to propose, in French, the toast of "The Arts and Monsieur Oscar Wilde." Zola ended his speech with spleen. "Unfortunately, Monsieur Wilde will be able to reply in his own barbarous language. . . ." Wilde rose slowly to observe, "I am Irish by birth and English by adoption so that, alas, I am condemned to speak in the language of Shakespeare." Wilde was later to say of Zola, "Zola is determined to show that if he has not genius, he at least can be dull. And how well he succeeds!"

A frequent visitor to these Parisian bistro gatherings was Constant-Benoit Coquelin, darling of the Comédie Française and creator of Rostand's classic *Cyrano de Bergerac*, who asked Wilde about *The Duchess of Padua*. Wilde explained that the play was solely an exercise of style, adding, "Between them Victor Hugo and Shakespeare have exhausted every subject. Originality is no longer possible, even in sin. So there are no real emotions left—only extraordinary adjectives!"

Coquelin, author of two major books on acting, much admired Wilde and questioned him on aspects of the writer's personal philosophy. "What is civilization, Monsieur Wilde?" "Love of beauty," came the answer. "And what is beauty?" "That which the bourgeois call ugly." "And what do the bourgeois call beautiful?" pursued Coquelin. "It does not exist," said Wilde.

Later, as Wilde was surrounded by Verlaine, Jean Richepin, Pissarro, and others, the conversation changed from beauty to ugliness, of which he had an enduring horror. And he let his revulsion be known. "It is better to be beautiful than to be good," he pronounced, "but it is better to be good than to be ugly." And had he not earlier said, "I consider ugliness a kind of malady, and illness and suffering inspire me with revulsion. A man with the toothache ought, I know, to have my sympathy for it is a terrible pain, yet he fills me with nothing but aversion?"

On his return to London, Wilde's mild output of work had produced a decidedly impoverished state of affairs. His finances were next to nil; he had spent the $1,000 advance from Mary Anderson for *The Duchess of Padua*, and because of its rejection, Wilde had seen nothing of the contracted $3,000 to be paid to him on delivery and acceptance. There was only one thing left to do to improve his impecuniosity: go on another lecture tour. Perhaps it was prophetic when earlier, in the Café Royal, he had held that "It is only by not paying one's bills that one can hope to live in the memory of the commercial classes!"

Colonel Morse, the administrator of the D'Oyly Carte Company, who produced the Gilbert and Sullivan operas, had originally sent him to America to promote the company's operetta *Patience*. A shrewd gamble, it had paid off, and Morse was warmly disposed towards Wilde. He promised to fix up a further lecture tour—this time in England and Scotland.

Before undertaking this tour, Wilde wanted to hasten things up with *Vera, or The Nihilists*, which was in rehearsal in America with actress Mary Prescott in the lead. He decided on a quick trip to the States. The play opened in New York in August 1883, and Wilde was present at the opening in his usual flamboyant attire. The play was a resounding flop, running exactly one week.

Determined to reestablish his fortunes, Wilde returned to start his British lecture tour. He decided that the content of his lectures should be based on his recent American experiences. After all, if the Americans had laughed at the British way of life in terms of Wildean Aestheticism, why not vice versa? Why not, indeed!

"I would rather have discovered Mrs. Lily Langtry than have discovered America," he explained. And for British edification, he described Niagara Falls as "simply a vast unnecessary amount of water going the wrong way and then falling over unnecessary rocks."

He referred, too, to the unusual American way of hanging pictures. He had remarked on this in San Francisco, with considerable resultant press coverage.

"The habit in America of hanging pictures up near the cornice struck me as irrational at first. It was not until I saw how bad the pictures were that I realized the advantage of the custom!" And he irreverently quipped, "Of course, America had often been discovered before Columbus, but it had always been hushed up!"

Other aspects of American life brought forth these observations, to the delight of his audiences:

"I believe a most serious problem for the American people to consider is the cultivation of better manners. It is the most noticeable, the most painful defect in American civilization." And, "There are few trappings, no pageants and no striking ceremonies in America. I saw only two processions: the Fire Brigade preceded by the Police and the Police preceded by the

Fire Brigade." And what of the fabled American railway system? "Everybody over there seems to be in a hurry to catch a train—a state of affairs not favorable to poetry or romance. . . ."

Wilde was never at a loss. When asked to comment further on his impressions of American women, he expressed the view, "Pretty and charming; little oases of pretty unreasonableness in a vast desert of practical common sense." The youth of America, too, came in for some characteristic comment. ". . . youth is America's oldest tradition. It has been going on now for three hundred years. To hear them talk we would imagine they were in their first childhood. As far as civilization goes, they are in their second."

The tour ended. Wilde's bank balance had taken on a healthier gleam.

SIN, SANCTITY, AND SOPHISTRY

True wit, to every man, is that which falls on another
— WALTER SAVAGE LANDOR, "Alexander and the Priest of Hammon," *Imaginary Conversations*, 1824

Oscar Wilde's wit and humor were totally matchless. He had no peers. Not even Bernard Shaw could surpass or even equal him. Earlier, Sydney Smith, cleric, brilliant conversationalist, and aphorist, was Oscar's nearest nineteenth-century rival, with Wilde's contemporary, James McNeill Whistler—he who immortalized his mother in paint—a close runner-up. Those who tried to imitate Wilde's genius for the barbed bon mot, the deadly-aimed aphorism, and the mordant paradox were, as Hesketh Pearson said, to be dismissed as "Wilde and water!"

His brilliance as a raconteur was pre-eminent; he could go on for hours at a time. Ever-changing circles of admirers would plead with him to continue, even when he was obviously tiring. His impressive appearance, combined with deft delivery and controlled facial expression, all contributed to his skill.

His many biographers agree that it was unknown for him to deliver a line or indeed a word invested with personal hate, spite, or viciousness. He was the master of satire—but, as well he knew, satire is only at its most biting when it is based on truth. If malice was apparent in others, he would invariably feign a look of pained indignation mixed with an air of assumed pity, and as likely as not throw away a comment such as, "It is perfectly monstrous, and quite heartless, the way people go about nowadays saying things against one, behind one's back, that are absolutely and entirely . . . true!"

His coruscating wit shone with great good humor. Dame Nellie Melba described it as "that brilliant fiery-colored chain of words." For most of us, try as we might to deliver even the occasional pseudo-Wildean riposte, we are invariably left to ponder the wisdom of Alexander Pope's truism, "You beat your pate, and fancy wit will come;/Knock as you please, there's nobody at home." ° Alternatively, we contemplate the truth of Jonathan Swift's shaft in his preface to *Tale of a Tub:* "It is with wits as with razors, which are never so apt to cut those they are employed on as when they have lost their edge. . . ."

That egregious twentieth-century wit, Lady Nancy Astor, might have gotten close to Wilde's secret of superb verbal dexterity when she claimed, "We women do talk too much, but even then we don't tell half we know!"

Part of Wilde's secret was his academic brilliance and knowledge of the world and its affairs—which were little short of prodigious—and his near-Oriental mask of assumed solemnity, which much of the time hid his ability to laugh at himself.

° *Epigram: An Empty House*

He was a luncheon guest of the Asquiths on 17 July 1894, two months after their marriage. By all accounts it was a scintillating gathering, peopled by some of the best minds of the day. Wilfred Scawen Blunt, himself a literary figure of magnitude who was in demand at many distinguished dinners and parties, recorded his impression of Wilde at this particular celebratory luncheon:

> Of all those present, and they were most of them brilliant talkers, Wilde was without comparison the most brilliant, and in a perverse mood he chose to cross swords with one after the other of the guests, overpowering each in turn with his wit, and making special fun of [Herbert] Asquith, his host that day who, only a few months later as Home Secretary of the Government, was prosecuting him. . . .

Later, Blunt in his diary added to this tribute.

> He was without exception the most brilliant talker I have ever come across, the most ready, the most witty, the most audacious . . . nobody could pretend to outshine him, or even to shine at all in his company. . . .

Hesketh Pearson nailed Wilde's technique. "His favorite method of ridiculing conventional standards was to change a word or two in a proverb or cliché and so add an aspect to truth." Not even Shakespeare, even in paraphrase, was sacrosanct to Wilde. "Nothing makes one so vain as being told one is a sinner. Conscience makes egotists of us all. . . ."

Coulson Kernahan, speaking with considerable conviction at a gathering, had just finished summarizing his deeply held religious beliefs when Oscar opined, "You are so evidently, so unmistakably sincere, and most of all so truthful, that . . . I can't believe a single word you say!" Another put-down must have smarted for weeks when Wilde, failing to recognize a gushing social climber who insisted that they had met in

Manchester, quipped, "Very possibly in Manchester I may know you again!"

On another occasion, Wilde found himself enlisted to escort a highbrow, po-faced woman into dinner. In an effort to make conversation, she chirruped tritely, "What terrible weather we are having." "Yes," said Wilde, "but if it wasn't for the snow how could we believe in the immortality of the soul?" The woman looked at him strangely. "What an interesting point of view, Mr. Wilde," she rejoined. "But tell me exactly what you mean?" Oscar was said to have raised his eyebrows slightly and replied, "I haven't the slightest idea!"

Many of Wilde's friends enjoyed repeating the story of the affluent foreign gentleman who by every means at his disposal tried to attract every London celebrity to his home. Wilde described him thus: "He came to London with the intention of opening a salon, and he has succeeded in opening a saloon." And the erstwhile Countess de Grey, she of the string of *affairs d'amour*, arrived at Oscar's home in Tite Street to be greeted by her host with, "My dear Countess—I'm so glad you've come. There are a hundred things I want not to say to you!"

He knew, too, the inherent truth of his words when, ever the iconoclast, he opined, "Man is least himself when he talks in his own person. Give him a mask and he will tell you the truth"; and on the subject of the troubled soul, this was his prescription: "Nothing can cure the soul but the senses, just as nothing can cure the senses but the soul"; while, laconically, "Genius is born, not paid."

In conversation with Laurence Housman, he opined, "Prayer must never be answered; if it is, it ceases to be prayer and becomes a correspondence. . . ." He held that "I do not approve of anything that tampers with natural ignorance." And his friend, the remarkable Ada Leverson, at a meeting in

1884, was assured that "God and other artists are always a little obscure."

There were other occasions when he would reveal a special kind of wisdom. "To believe is very dull. To doubt is intensely engrossing. To be on the alert is to live. To be lulled into security is to die." About this time, too, he bemoaned in the *Saturday Review* that "It is a very sad thing that nowadays there is so little useless information," and he scored a direct hit with, "Anyone can sympathize with the sufferings of a friend, but it requires a very fine nature to sympathize with a friend's success!"

Again in the *Saturday Review*, of 17 November 1894, he propounded, "One should never listen. To listen is a sign of indifference to one's hearers."

He regarded shallowness as a cardinal sin. This is strongly borne out by his penultimate manuscript, *De Profundis*, in which he accused "Bosie" Douglas, "Do not be afraid. The supreme vice is shallowness. Everything that is realised is right. Remember also that whatever is misery to you to read, is still greater misery to me to set down. . . ." Much earlier he had said, "Seriousness is the only refuge of the shallow."

There is little doubt that he had something of an obsession about age—more particularly his own age. In his verbal sallies, as in his writings, he turned frequently to youth, his favorite subject. While enjoying celebrity status, he remembered his undergraduate days thus: "When I filled in a census paper I gave my age as nineteen, my profession as genius, my infirmity as talent," a slice of impeccable self-mockery.

But recalling Plato's dictum, which he was fond of quoting at Oxford—"The highest end that man can attain here below is to sit down and contemplate the good"—he evolved a variation to witty effect: "To do nothing at all is the most difficult thing in the world, the most difficult and most intellectual."

Wilde was a "good touch" to penurious friends and acquaintances, although he conceded that "Charity creates a multitude of sins." Accosted one evening in London's Haymarket by a beggar who pleaded that he was workless and had no bread to eat, Wilde teasingly rejoined, "Work, why on earth should you want to work? And bread! Why should you eat bread?" Putting an arm around the man's shoulder, he continued his mock lesson in morality. "Now, if you had come to see me and said that you had work to do, but you couldn't dream of working, and that you had bread to eat, but shouldn't think of eating bread, I would have given you two shillings and sixpence." He paused for a moment, his smile becoming broader. "As it is," he said, "I'll give you half-a-crown!"

Wilde loved to work, but it is said that he loved leisure more. His leisure, however, rarely approached boredom. He confirmed this with, "The only horrible thing in the world is ennui. That is the only sin for which there is no forgiveness." He even paraphrased an aphorism that Mark Twain had apparently appropriated (and, incidentally, ruined!). Wilde claimed, "I never put off till tomorrow what I can possibly do . . . the day after!" But given the opportunity—and he was never short of opportunities—he was prepared to admit that "When people agree with me I always feel that I must be wrong!" He also held the opinion that "To know everything about oneself, one must know all about others," but did concede, "I am the only person in the world I should like to know thoroughly, but I don't see any chance of it just at present!" His mature air of sophistry, however, persuaded him to admit, "To be natural is such a very difficult pose to keep up."

On the subject of friends and enemies he was, as ever, masterly. "I choose my friends for their good looks, my acquaintances for their good characters, and my enemies for their good intellects. A man cannot be too careful in the choice of his enemies." Holding, too, that "It is only the intellectually lost who ever argue," he considered that "Conscience must be merged in instinct before we become fine: conscience and cowardice are really the same things—conscience is the trade-name of the firm."

On occasions, he was accused of arrogance.

The English mind [he wrote incisively] is always in a rage. The intellect of the race is wasted in the sordid and stupid quarrels of second-rate politicians and third-rate theologians . . . we are dominated by the fanatic, whose worst vice is his sincerity . . . there is no sin except stupidity.

He would frequently electrify his listeners with a shaft like this: "The reason we like to think well of others is that we are all afraid for ourselves. The basis of our optimism is sheer terror." And he admitted "There is luxury in self-reproach. When we blame ourselves we feel that no one else has a right to blame us. It is the confession, not the priest, that gives us absolution."

Returning to the subject of age, this twist of truth: "The tragedy of old age is not that one is old, but that one is not young"; and in similar vein, he held that "Young men want to be faithful, and are not; old men want to be faithless, and cannot."

Touching exposed nerves was his speciality. "Don't tell me," he once expostulated, "that you have exhausted Life. When a man says that, one knows that Life has exhausted him!" And Wilde loved to debunk the virtuous *poseur*. "Noth-ing," he claimed, "is more painful to me than to come across virtue in a person in whom I have never expected its existence. It is like finding a needle in a bundle of hay. It pricks you. If we have virtue we should warn people of it."

There is no Secret of Life. Life's aim, if it has one, is simply to be always looking for temptations. There are not nearly enough of them. I sometimes pass a whole day without coming across a single one. It is quite dreadful. It makes one so nervous about the future!

Wilde was in a conversation involving a young man who was being informed by an elder that, like everyone else he must begin his career at the bottom of the ladder. Moving in with characteristic assurance and aplomb, "No," he advised the youth, aiming straight for the jugular, "begin at the top and sit on it!" The elder protested that the lad was to join the Sandhurst Military Academy. Wilde tried to talk the youth out of it. "You must to go Oxford," he said. "But I am going to become a soldier," protested the youth. "In which case," said Oscar, "if you took a degree at Oxford, they would make you a Colonel at once," adding, as a smiling aside, "At any rate in a West Indian regiment!"

PROFESSOR OF AESTHETICS
AND LORD OF LANGUAGE

*When I hear a man applauded by the mob, I
always feel a pang of pity for him. All he has
to do to be hissed is to live long enough.*
—H. L. MENCKEN, *Minority Report*, 1856

A marvelous sense of fun runs through most Wildean words. Not without some trepidation, the British peer Lord Avebury had published a list of The Hundred Best Books. At a function to launch the selection, Wilde was invited to submit *his* list. "I fear that would be impossible," he said. "I have only written five!"

In Victorian times—and the habit lingers still—women were expected to leave the dining table before the men, who would remain to light their cigars, drink port, and exchange risqué stories. At one such party, largely because of Wilde's own captivating talk, the ladies lingered a little too long. A table lamp began to smolder. The hostess grew concerned. "Please put it out, Mr. Wilde," she requested, "I fear it's smoking." "Happy lamp!" murmured Wilde.

Wilde's sense of satire rarely deserted him, even in the later tortuous stages of his life. Periodically he would return to his two favorite topics—youth and age. Talking to a young writer, he held forth for some time on the enchantment of being young, on the glories of adolescence. He concluded "To win back my youth there is nothing I would not do—nothing . . . except take exercise, get up early, or be a useful member of the community!"

One day, walking with Frank Harris along the fashionable London thoroughfare of Jermyn Street, St. James's, Wilde espied an elegant florist shop; both men entered. A saleslady approached, and Oscar asked her to remove several flower displays from the window.

"With pleasure, Sir. Will you take them or shall I send them?" "Oh," exclaimed Wilde with an air of faint disdain, "I don't want any, thank you. I only asked to have them removed from the window because I thought they looked a trifle tired!"

He equated ignorance to a delicate, exotic fruit; "Touch it and the bloom is gone." And at a Burlington House, London, art exhibition preview, he let it be known that, in his opinion, "Nature is elbowing her way into the charmed circle of Art."

It has been claimed by Professor Richard Ellmann that Wilde would have concurred with Nabokov that "art is a kind of trick played on nature," or "If art be a mirror"—as was claimed by Hamlet—"we look into it to see—a mask." Wilde might equally have observed that "Nature is a kind of trick played on art."

Another of his favorite subjects—temptation—frequently cropped up in his conversation. He explained, "Every impulse that we strive to strangle broods in the mind and poisons us . . . the only way to get rid of temptation is to yield to it!"

Often acidulous about certain people, his observations were invariably laced with laughter, as when he said of one of the Café Royal circle, "He hasn't a single redeeming vice!"

He was called on to prove his jesting boast that he could talk on any subject. A cry went up from his coterie. "The Queen! The Queen! Talk about the Queen, Oscar!" With barely a pause, he smiled and said, "The Queen is not a subject!"

Early in his life, and even when riding the crest of his fame, Wilde had a strange preoccupation with the criminal classes. Murder, of course, motivates *The Picture of Dorian Gray,* and "Lord Arthur Savile's Crime" satirizes and conceals it. In his essay "The Soul of Man Under Socialism," he considered that "Crime . . . under certain conditions, may be said to have created individualism." And he went further: "Wickedness is a myth invented by good people to account for the curious attractiveness of others."

Perhaps, like many artists, Wilde was disturbed by a recurring premonition of his own destiny. In any event, he held pronounced views on crime and criminals. At the end of 1894 in the *Saturday Review,* he wrote, "The criminal classes are so close to us that even the policemen can see them. They are so far away from us that only the poet can understand them." And he was prepared to admit that "Society produces rogues, and education makes one rogue cleverer than another," but seemed certain about the criminals' lack of capacity to reach higher plateaux: "Art is rarely intelligible to the criminal classes." He admitted, "I can stand brute force, but brute reason is quite unbearable. There is something unfair about its use. It is hitting below the intellect."

Wilde had scant regard for the historical fairness of the individual or the judiciary.

> As one reads history . . . one is absolutely sickened, not by the crimes that the wicked have committed, but by the punishments that the good have inflicted. And a community is infinitely more brutalised by the habitual employment of punishment than it is by the occasional occurences of crime.

I am not at all sure that even the most erudite criminologist would have accepted Wilde's cleverly-argued theory in its application to the modern world and, no doubt, he would have modified or even changed his approach in the twentieth-century age of hijackings and spiraling world violence. Be that as it may, the artist should be heard, and Wilde was never one to display reticence in projecting his original thinking on any subject.

In Victorian times, as today, lawyers came in for plenty of criticism, often not without reason. They displayed then, as they frequently display today, "an insatiable appetite for fees" within a structure of a veiled "trade union" which possesses the tightest closed-shop policy in Christendom. Thus, they must be prepared to accept criticism, satire and even derision.

There was the classic Note of Fees system for charging clients which appeared after a bill and been "taxed" by that strange, mysterious body known in legal circles as Taxing Masters, a cloisteral conclave of faceless fiscal dictators. During Wilde's time, there was a much-publicized Note of Fees affair that caused great amusement. A bill was rendered "To crossing the Strand after seeing you on the other side, to discuss your case with you: Six Shillings and Eightpence." On reading this devious document, Wilde thought he would have fun with Theodore Watts-Dunton, who happened to be a poet, novelist, a friend of Bosie Douglas and Swinburne—and a solicitor to boot. "I have suddenly realised," said Wilde to a close friend, "why Watts-Dunton is an authority on the sonnet form . . . it is, of course, made of six and eight!"

His reaction to newspapers was acerbic: "Newspapers have degenerated; they may now be absolutely relied on!" And he abhorred the practice that "At present the newspapers are trying hard to induce the public to judge a sculptor, for instance, never by his statues but by the way he treats his wife; a painter by the amount of his income; and a poet by the colour of his necktie." Times change, but evidently newspapers don't.

Being Wilde, he sometimes twisted the tail of truth. "All fine imaginative work is self-conscious and deliberate. A great poet sings because he chooses to sing. On the other hand, if one tells the truth one is sure, sooner or later, to be found out!"

Eccentricity, it has been said, is often the sign of a superior intelligence, and Wilde, at this stage of his life and career, was becoming markedly more eccentric, both in dress and social habits. His heavy features betrayed his delight in the almost alarmed reaction of the masses to his outlandish, but always elegant, attire. His frivolity was ever apparent, and as Pearson has said, "good nature seemed to exude from him, pleasure to radiate from him, happiness to enfold him."

When Wilde affected profundity one could be certain it was mixed with an underlying sense of fun. His assured demeanor would, by a single smiling gesture, indicate "the degree of significance he attached to whatever epigram or paradox he had just delivered."

It was Wilde's opinion that "Humanity takes itself too seriously. It is the world's original sin. If the caveman had known how to laugh, history would have been different." No doubt he was right; the humorist is invariably the most perceptive of men: witness Wilde's remark, "Whenever I think of my bad qualities at night, I go to sleep at once"; or, "I am due at my club. It is the hour when we sleep there."

He took the view, too, that "Morality is simply the attitude we adopt towards people we personally dislike," and his consideration for the artist was always apparent: "For an artist to marry his model is as fatal as for a gourmet to marry his cook: the one gets no sittings, and the other no dinners!"

About modernity he was crisp, paradoxical and pointed: "Nothing is so dangerous as being too modern. One is apt to grow old-fashioned quite suddenly."

And if brevity be the soul of wit, Wilde was its essence. "I rely on you to misrepresent me!" he once said, and, speaking of an acquaintance, "He is old enough to know worse."

It follows that his manner and delivery contributed much towards the actual wit of his words, and his formidable height and frame, no less than his dress, added greatly to his impact. He could be stern as well as funny. "We are not sent into this world to air our moral prejudices," he once said with an air of assumed detachment, adding, "What people call insincerity is simply a method by which we can multiply our personalities."

Wilde and his words were invariably a coruscating combination of the unexpected: "A cynic is a man who knows the price of everything and the value of nothing." If during his lifetime he had uttered no more than that single epigram, he would today be remembered for it. But he was to go on and on, in plays, books, articles, critiques and essays. "I must decline your invitation due to a subsequent engagement!" is surely the most tactful, if uncomplimentary, way of refusing an invitation. Although he often pretended not to give advice, he repeatedly did so under a veil of hilarious paradox, as with "It is always a silly thing to give advice, but to give good advice is absolutely fatal." Similarly, "It is only about the things that do not interest one that one can give an unbiased opinion; this is no doubt the reason why an unbiased opinion is always valueless!"

He liked to travel but couldn't refrain from commenting, "Of what use is it to a man to travel sixty miles an hour? Is he any the better for it? Why, a fool can buy a railway ticket and travel at sixty miles an hour. Is he any the less a fool?" And he is on record as saying, "I would sooner lose a train by the ABC than catch it by Bradshaw." ° He also had this to say about the commercial amenities of his day: "People should not mistake the means of civilisation for the end. The steam engine and the telephone depend entirely for their value on the use to which they are put." On another occasion, he similarly held that "The value of the telephone is the value of what two people have to say to each other."

On the social scene, he was sometimes merciless, but always direct. "A gentleman is one who never hurts anyone's feelings unintentionally!"

At the height of his fame he adored socializing, though later on, he came to despise the salon scene and all it stood for. During his period as "the literary lion," he angered and amused London's hosts and hostesses with "To get into the best society nowadays one has either to feed people, amuse people, or shock people—that is all!" And he couldn't resist a dig at "the City Establishment:" "With an evening coat and a white tie, anybody—even a stockbroker—can gain a reputation for being civilised!"

Although Wilde loved good talk, he disliked unseemly argument. "Arguments are to be avoided," he claimed, "they are always vulgar and often convincing!" And on a similar theme he was risibly rhetorical: "Arguments are extremely vulgar, for everybody in good society holds exactly the same opinions." He knew, too, that most people have a public and a private face; hence, "Most people are other people. Their thoughts are someone else's opinions, their lives a mimicry, their passions merely a quotation." He further averred, "I am very fond of the public; personally I always patronise the public very much!"; and he made no bones about his view that

---

° The ABC in Wilde's time, was the *official* railway timetable; Bradshaw's Guide was a similar directory of times and routes published by a commercial firm, reliable but "non-official."

"The first duty of life is to be as artificial as possible; what the second duty is, no one has yet discovered!"

Others were scant match for him. He assumed a disdainful air towards most politicians, despite the fact that he numbered Prime Minister Arthur Balfour among his close friends. But both Upper and Lower Houses of the British Parliament found little support from him. If pressed, he would probably have admitted that he was no exception to the adage that "Everybody Loves a Lord." At all events, he once delivered this homily: "The Lords Temporal say nothing; the Lords Spiritual ° have nothing to say; and the House of Commons has nothing to say and says it!"

Although his charmed circle included many peers, statesmen, politicians, and noblemen, he was not one to tolerate the coarse slap on the back as a form of greeting. On one occasion, in the middle of a Wildean conversational toehold, a nobleman did so slap him in exuberant greeting, exlaiming, "Why, Oscar, you are getting fatter and fatter!" To which Wilde, with cold disdain, rejoined, "And you, sir, are getting ruder and ruder!"

On another occasion, a bucolic individual dug him in the ribs, greeting him with, "Hello, Oscar!" Wilde turned slowly to the man and with disarming hauteur replied, "I don't know you by sight, but your manner is familiar. . . ."

Once discussing the desirability of politicians being painted in oils for posterity, his indignation was warmed by a smile as he pontificated, "There is hardly a single person in the House of Commons worth painting, though many of them would be the better for a little whitewashing!"

Arthur Balfour once asked Wilde about his religious beliefs. Oscar replied, "Well, you know, my dear Arthur, I don't think I have any. I am an Irish Protestant."

° The Lords Spiritual are Church of England archbishops and bishops.

He frequently claimed, "The public will forgive anything except genius," but his close circle of friends were ever ready to forgive him an occasional memory lapse if momentarily he forgot a face. On one occasion when this happened to an old acquaintance, Oscar was equal to the challenge. "My dear fellow," he drawled, "do forgive me, I didn't recognize you— I've changed a lot!"

Discussing personal hygiene with the notorious "Master of Black Magic," Alester Crowley, at the Café Royal, he said, "I know so many men in London whose only talent is for washing. I suppose that is why men of genius so seldom wash—they are afraid of being mistaken for men of talent only!"

At the same venue, he was discussing an unfortunate fracas between two of his friends. It seems that things had gotten out of hand. Wilde took up the story. ". . . Robert gave Harry a terrible black eye, or Harry gave him one—I forget which—but I know they were great friends!"

He frequently deplored the duplicity of man, as when he said, "We think that we are generous because we credit our neighbour with the possession of those virtues that are likely to be a benefit to us," and his cynicism was well to the fore when he claimed, "The gratitude of most men is but a secret desire of receiving greater benefits."

It has been said that Wilde, behind all his sophistry, was sentimental. Did he mean it, then, when he said, "The sentimentalist is always a cynic at heart. Indeed, sentimentality is merely the Bank Holiday of cynicism?"

Science and scientists were anathema to him. "Science," he claimed, "can never grapple with the irrational. That is why it has no future before it in this world." This, of course, was the artist speaking, and doubtless the scientists chuckled and kept their heads well down. As, too, those to whom this applied: "Good resolutions are simply cheques that men draw on a bank where they have no account!"

On the female of the species, as we shall see, he had *much* to say, not least: "When a woman marries again it is because she detested her first husband. When a man marries again it is because he adored his first wife. Women try their luck; men risk theirs!"

There were, of course, those who could be satirically venomous about Oscar. Max Beerbohm was a case in point; he summed up Oscar in these clipped words:

Luxury — gold-tipped matches — hair curled — Assyrian — wax statue — huge rings — fat white hands — not soigné — feather bed — pointed fingers — ample scarf — Louis Quinze cane — vast Malmaison — cat-like tread — heavy shoulders — enormous dowager — or schoolboy — way of laughing with hand over mouth — stroking chin — looking up sideways — jollity overdone — but real vitality —

A cruel assessment, but one that troubled Oscar not one whit. Especially when he learned that these were Max's notes for a projected literary portrait of him!

WILDE ABOUT WOMEN

Woman: the peg on which the wit hangs his
jest, the preacher his text, the cynic his grouch,
and the sinner his justification
                              —HELEN ROWLAND (1875-1950)

Oscar Wilde, the toast of his age, enjoyed a reputation among women that men envied. Women in society circles of the late nineteenth century adored him; they sought to entertain him; they hung on his every word and laughed endlessly at his wit. He, too, patently enjoyed their company.

If he really believed that "Women try their luck; men risk theirs in marriage," it made little difference to his devotion to love. "Each time one loves," he said, "is the only time that one has ever loved. Difference of object does not alter singleness of passion. It merely intensifies it."

If that sounds a trifle superficial, listen again to Wilde the man who, throughout his life was visually and vocally in love with Beauty: "More women grow old nowadays through the faithfulness of their admirers than through anything else."

And he acidulously observed of a certain female charmer in his circle, "When she is in a very smart gown, she looks like an *'edition de luxe'* of a wicked French novel meant specially for the English market." His iconoclasm rarely failed him. "Twenty years of romance makes a woman look like a ruin; but twenty years of marriage makes her something like a public building!"

Complete with a droplet of vitriol laced with a puff of pomade, he described another female of his acquaintance. "She is without one good quality; she lacks the tinest spark of decency, and is quite the wickedest woman in London. I haven't a word to say in her favour—and she is one of my greatest friends!" Of another well-known beauty he claimed, "Her capacity for family affection is extraordinary. When her third husband died her hair turned quite gold from grief!"

He observed with accuracy of his garrulous and opinionated friend, Ouida, "Ouida loved Lord Lytton with a love that made his life a burden"; and of yet another woman in his charmed circle, he declared, "She has the remains of really remarkable ugliness!"

He had, too, this piece of general advice: "Don't be led astray into the paths of virtue." And he is on record as claiming, "I have never given adoration to anyone except myself!"

He might thus be forgiven for having written in "The Sphinx," "Women are meant to be loved, not to be understood." Most feminine techniques he also well knew. "Woman begins by resisting a man's advances and ends by blocking his retreat!"

His witticisms on women sprouted like mushrooms after rain. This of a well-known socialite: "She is a peacock in everything but beauty." On the same occasion he observed that "A woman with a past has no future!"

That may have been valid in his day, but it is unlikely to strike a chord of approval in today's permissive society. But his cut that "Modern women understand everything except their husbands" is likely to find a responsive chord among many males of the twentieth century. At worst—or best—he deserves a prolonged "bravo" for his observation, "Women have a much better time than men in this world; there are far more things forbidden to them!"

His approach to the question of age finds an echo in this quip designed for consumption exclusively by women: "No women should ever be quite accurate about her age—it looks so calculating!"

Speaking of another female, he observed, "Immoral women are rarely attractive—what made her quite irresistible was that she was unmoral . . ."; and he seemed to applaud the fact that "Women have been so highly-educated that nothing should surprise them except happy marriages."

Wilde *could* be serious on occasions, as when he expounded, "When there is no exaggeration there is no love, and where there is no love, there is no understanding." And "She who hesitates is won" can, for the lusting male, brook no argument!

Wilde doubted the attractions of polygamy but, as usual, he had an answer. "How much more poetic it is to marry one and love many!" His clipped observation "Divorces are made in heaven" hardly stands up to today's the legal trends, but there's an element of fundamental wisdom in his advice, "Talk to every woman as if you loved her, and to every man as if he bored you." And many will consider he scored a bull's-eye with "The worst of having a romance of any kind is that it leaves one so unromantic!"

Oscar, being Oscar, could—and did—delight both women and men with this Tite Street homily: "The amount of women in London who flirt with their own husbands is perfectly scandalous. It looks so bad! It is simply washing one's clean linen in public!" And, "Women," he once roundly declared, "represent the triumph of matter over mind, just as men represent the triumph over morals!" That needs quite a bit of dissecting, doesn't it?

Although Oscar Wilde's marriage to Constance appeared successful—at least until his unhappy trials—he wickedly observed of the institution, "The one charm of marriage is that it makes life a deception absolutely necessary for both parties."

He was normally the soul of courtesy towards Constance, but his bubbling wit never flagged, even occasionally at her expense. At a Tite Street dinner party, Oscar, holding sway, stood and took up the carvers to slice a chicken for his guests. He tried to separate a wing from the carcass, was unsuccessful, and, laying down the carvers with a weary gesture, upbraided his wife, "Constance, why do you give me these . . . pedestrians to eat?" The answer given by Constance is not on record.

What *is* on record is yet another astringent witticism on the subject of marriage; trust him to find a joker in the pack. "It is a curious thing about the game of marriage," he said, "the wives hold all the honors and invariably lose the last trick!

On another occasion he observed, no less wearily, "Married life is merely a habit," and underlined this by a subsequent solecism, "In married households the champagne is rarely of a first-rate brand."

Women connoted domesticity and domesticity financial burdens. Oscar's persistent money problems culminated one day with the arrival of a taxman on his Tite Street doorstep.

"I have called about your taxes," said the little man. Wilde looked haughty and remonstrated, "Taxes! Why should I pay taxes?" "But, sir," protested the man, "you are the householder here, are you not? You live here, you sleep here . . ." "Ah, yes," parried Oscar, "but then, you see, I sleep so badly. . . ."

Oscar never faltered when in full flood, especially when

women were present, as when he delivered this broadside: "Crying is the refuge of plain women but the ruin of pretty ones."

He was emphatic when he smilingly belaboured an audience with "Women treat us men just as humanity treats its gods. They worship us—and are always bothering us to do something for them." And who would argue with his cynical opinion that "A man can be happy with any woman as long as he does not love her"?

Wilde did not confine his observations on the feminine sex to dinner parties and plays. In November 1894, in the *Saturday Review*, he penned this salutary thought: "Most women are so artificial that they have no sense of Art. Most men are so natural that they have no sense of beauty"; and, in the same piece, with equal cynicism, held that "Friendship is more tragic than love. It lasts longer!"

Little about feminine wiles eluded him. He once argued in an article on "Suitable Dress for Women Workers," "After all, what is fashion? From the artistic point of view it is usually a form of ugliness so intolerable that we have to change it every six months!" Not finished on the subject of fashion, he once roundly declared, "Women's styles may change but their designs remain the same!" How true!

It was the same taste of truth he injected into Act 1 of *An Ideal Husband*, in which he reminded us, "You know what a woman's curiosity is—almost as great as a man's!"

A DISTINCTIVE DISTILLATION

I fear nothing so much as a man who is witty
all day long

—MADAME DE SÉVIGNÉ (1626-1696)

During the forty-six years of his life, and particularly during the ten years of his prolific literary output, Oscar Wilde expressed countless thoughts, many unrelated to Aestheticism. These have since become immortalized, along with his better-known sayings, in text books, collections, and anthologies; many have inevitably found their way into the Pattern of Language, the Color of Saying.

Here, then, on diverse subjects, is a distinctive distillation, a cross-section of those epigrams, paradoxes, adages, and maxims.

Acidity

Nowadays all married men live like bachelors and all bachelors live like married men.

Admiration

Bad artists always admire each other's work.

Appearances

One can always recognise women who trust their husbands; they look so thoroughly unhappy.

Arguments

Marriage is one subject on which all women agree and all men disagree.

Artistic

The true artist is known by the use he makes of what he annexes, and he annexes everything.

Bachelors

By persistently remaining single, a man converts himself into a permanent public temptation.

Beauty

A subject that is beautiful in itself gives no suggestion to the artist. It lacks imperfection.

Behavior

He doesn't act on the stage—he behaves. . . .

Beliefs

Man can believe the impossible, but man can never believe the improbable.

Cynicism

When a man has once loved a woman, he will do anything for her, except continue to love her.

Disappointments

Niagara Falls is only the second biggest disappointment of the standard honeymoon.

Equanimity

Philosophy teaches us to bear with equanimity the misfortunes of others.

Fanaticism

The worst vice of the fanatic is his sincerity.

Generosity

Women give to men the very gold of their lives. But they invariably want it back in small change.

Hypocrisy

I hope you have not been leading a double life, pretending to be wicked, and being really good all the time. That would be hypocrisy.

Ignorance

For he, to whom the present is the only thing that is present, knows nothing of the age in which he lives.

Immorality

The books that the world calls immoral are the books that show the world its own shame.

Insincerity

The more insincere the man is, the more purely intellectual will the idea be as in that case it will not be coloured by either his wants, desires or his prejudices.

Legacy

It is enough that our fathers have believed. They have exhausted the faith-faculty of the species. Their legacy to us is the scepticism of which they were afraid.

Loving

One should always be in love. That is the reason one should never marry.

Lying

The only form of lying that is absolutely beyond reproach is lying for its own sake.

Marriages

Men marry because they are tired; women because they are curious. Both are disappointed.

Narcissism

To love oneself is the beginning of a lifelong romance.

Nourishment

Town life nourishes and perfects all the more civilised elements in man.

Optimism

The basis of optimism is sheer terror.

Patriotism

Patriotism is the virtue of the vicious.

Perfection

The true perfection of man lies, not in what he has, but in what he is.

Philosophy

A man who desires to get married should either know everything or nothing.

Poetry

There are two ways of disliking poetry: one way is to dislike it, the other is to read Pope.

Praiseworthy

The only thing that ever consoles man for the stupid things he does is the praise he always gives himself for doing them.

Preferences

A bad man is the sort of man who admires innocence, and a bad woman is the sort of woman a man never gets tired of.

Rashness

If one puts forward an idea to a true Englishman—always a rash thing to do—he never dreams of considering whether the idea is right or wrong. The only thing he considers of any importance is whether one believes it oneself.

Rationality

One is tempted to define man as a rational animal who always loses his temper when he is called upon to act in accordance with the dictates of reason.

Reaction

On Dickens: One must have a heart of stone to read the death of Little Nell without laughing.

Reading

We live in an age that reads too much to be wise.

Refuge

Consistency is the last refuge of the unimaginative.

Regrets

One's only real life is the life one never leads.

Resources

Action is the last resource of those who know not how to dream.

Rulers

No man has any real success in this world unless he has got a woman to back him, and women rule society.

Shallowness

Only the shallow know themselves.

Sincerity

The value of an idea has nothing whatsoever to do with the sincerity of the man who expresses it.

Tragedies

In the world there are only two tragedies. One is not getting what one wants, and the other is getting it.

Wastage

> The vilest deeds like poison weeds
> Bloom well in prison-air:
> It is only what is good in Man
> That wastes and withers there. . . .

Workaholics

Work is the refuge of people who have nothing better to do.

Writings

There is no such thing as a moral or an immoral book. Books are well written or badly written.

CURTAIN UP ON
LADY WINDERMERE

Wit lives in the present, but genius survives in the future.
> —Countess of Blessington (1789-1849)

Over the centuries, from Athenian drama—and even earlier—on through Lyly, Goldsmith, Wycherley, Congreve, Sheridan and, latterly, Synge, O'Casey, Shaw, Coward, and Ayckbourn, the theatre has boasted its quota of superior wits; none, I suggest, as scintillatingly original as Oscar Wilde.

Today, it remains richly rewarding to watch or read the mannered elegance of costumed comedy *à la* Wilde. His pursuit of perfection in Art is as much evident in terms of the high humor of his sophisticated Victorian drawing-room comedy as it is in his strange but absorbing work, *The Picture of Dorian Gray.*

Wilde's pursuit of perfection was not limited to the confines of the theater; it is evident in most of his writings and in most of his relationships. Although he professed his enduring love for Lily Langtry, his ardor was directed not so much at the woman herself as at her breathtaking, perfectionist beauty. And the sheaves of lilies he adoringly presented to Sarah Bernhardt (who replaced Lily in the affections of Bertie, Prince of Wales), were mainly in tribute to the actress, her beauty, and Art, and not to the woman as such.

True, such ostentatious and theatrical adoration was to a large extent expected of Wilde, but he behaved as he did primarily because he idolized the image of perfection so exquisitely represented by both Langtry and Bernhardt.

He found a rewarding response to his work within the theater and its disciples, and so he frequently entertained the greatest actors, actresses, and actor-managers of his time. They constituted part of *his* audience in the same way that he gathered around him poets, painters, and other creative beings from most areas of the arts; they, too were catalysts to his genius.

Like the elitist extrovert that he was, he found the theater vastly amusing, an ideal setting for his aphoristic dialogue, his sybaritic characters, his verbal cut-and-thrust; it was a near-perfect ambience in which to introduce the public to the inner world of Wilde. He used the theater as an extension of his salon, an extension to accommodate and disperse his gift of satire and other skills.

George Alexander, the actor-manager, was known for his business acumen; as an impresario he was an astute and clever bargainer. Wilde sent him the typescript of *Lady Windermere's Fan*. Alexander gave him an advance of £100 and tried to convince him that he ought to sell him the play on an outright basis—the full copyright—for £1,000. But Wilde, despite his dandyish manner, was usually astute when it came to business matters. He pretended to give the proposal his consideration and in due course delivered his reply. "My dear Alex," he wrote, "I have so much confidence in your excellent judgement that I cannot but refuse your most generous offer!"

It is well that he did; the play opened to a huge ovation and went on to make a fortune.

Lady Windermere's Fan, his first major theatrical success, opened on Saturday, 20 February 1892, to a brilliantly fashionable first night at the St. James's Theatre, London. George Alexander played Lord Windermere, and Lily Hanbury was Lady Windermere. Marion Terry was Mrs. Erlynne, and stalwarts like Nutcombe Gould, A. Vane Tempest, and Ben Webster all contributed to the overwhelming acclaim received by the play at the final curtain. Thus, Wilde joined Henry Arthur Jones and Arthur Wing Pinero in the top trio of contemporary playwrights.

Oscar—assured, immaculate and happy, cigarette dangling in a long holder—delivered his curtain speech to the delight of his followers. The critics, almost to a man, tried to damn the play with a torrent of faint praise, but their verdicts made no difference. Word-of-mouth praise transported it into a huge, commercial success.

During rehearsals, Wilde told Ben Webster, who was playing the role of Cecil Graham, that he should wear a green carnation in his buttonhole. "Green," asked Webster incredulously, "why on earth green?" "Because," said Oscar, "it is such a delightful colour." "But green carnations do not exist," said Webster. "True," agreed Wilde, "but they will; Nature always copies Art and it is our duty to teach Nature how to behave." Carnations were dyed for the purpose. And thus the green carnation became the Wildean symbol to all his acolytes.

Two petulant and jealous authors took time off to deride the play in a satirical pastiche called *The Poet and The Puppets,* which opened and closed at the nearby Comedy Theatre in Panton Street, Haymarket, in the space of a fortnight. The publicity it derived only helped to benefit *Lady Windermere's Fan.*

Wilde was the toast of the town, quoted wherever theatregoers and dilettantes gathered. How could one resist dialogue from *Lady Windermere's Fan* like, "A man who moralises is usually a hypocrite, and a woman who moralises is invariably plain"; or, "Men become old, but they never become good"; and, in an even more sardonic vein, "Between men and women there is no friendship possible. There is passion, enmity, worship, love—but no friendship."

He was, too, at his most acerbic with "It takes a thoroughly good woman to do a thoroughly stupid thing." And his exclamatory "How hard good women are! How weak bad men are!" positively charmed his elegant audiences.

Applause, too, greeted "Nowadays, we are all of us so hard up that the only pleasant things left to pay are compliments. They're the only things we can pay!" He might have been referring to inflationary times to follow!

Characteristically, he homed in again on his familiar theme of Scarlet Women—"I prefer women with a past. They're always so damned amusing to talk to!"—and, underlining this, quipped, "Wicked women bother one. Good women bore one. That is the only difference between them!"

Even his extended assessment of good and bad women, laced with seriousness, was greeted with laughter and applause.

> I don't think now that people can be divided into the good and the bad as though they were two separate races or creatures. What are called good women may have terrible things in them—mad moods of recklessness, assertion, jealousy, sin. Bad women, as they are termed, may have in in them sorrow, repentance, pity, sacrifice. . . .

With some truth, he also observed, "If a woman really repents, she never wishes to return to the society that has made or seen her ruined. . . ."

It was also in *Lady Windermere's Fan* that with classic clarity he admitted, "I can resist anything except temptation!" but, as was often the case, he'd said that before in salon conversation and simply transposed it for the theater.

His exhortations against the married state stippled all four acts of the play—"How marriage ruins a man! It's as demoralising as cigarettes, and far more expensive!"

Redemption occasionally overtook one of his characters—"As a wicked man I am a complete failure. Why, there are lots of people who say I have never really done anything wrong in the whole course of my life. Of course, they only say it behind my back!"

In this play as well, Wilde reveled in the paradox—"If you pretend to be good, the world takes you very seriously. If you pretend to be bad, it doesn't. Such is the astounding stupidity of optimism." But even in high comedy, Wilde had his occasional serious moment—"There's nothing in the world like the devotion of a married woman. It's a thing no married man knows anything about."

Earlier in the play, he held, "It is a dangerous thing to reform anyone!"

While *Lady Windermere's Fan* was enjoying its success, Wilde was asked whether he wrote the play with a specific leading actor in mind. He told his inquirer, "I never write plays for anyone in particular. I write to amuse myself. Later, if anyone wants to act in them, I sometimes allow them to do so!"

About this time, another happy landmark occurred in his career. Having had censorhsip trouble with *Salomé*, the censor having refused it a license because of the presence of biblical characters, he now enjoyed the pleasure of seeing its wide distribution in book form, beautifully decorated by his sensuous Café Royal acolyte, Aubrey Beardsley. It was an extravagant one-acter, originally written by him in French, in which Bernhardt had agreed to play the lead. It is perhaps best known today through Richard Strauss's opera of the same name, based on Wilde's original book.

But to return to *Lady Windermere's Fan*. Act I of the play projected this pregnant thought: "Life is far too important a thing ever to talk seriously about." And in the same Act, the irrepressible Oscar considered that "Experience is the name everyone gives to his mistakes!"

There was indignation, too, in "It is perfectly brutal the way most women nowadays behave to men who are not their husbands!" And he thought, "It is absurd to divide people into good and bad. People are either charming or tedious."

His pride in the spoken word undoubtedly inspired the line, "Nowadays, to be intelligible is to be found out!"

Happiness enfolded him like a blanket on a cold night. In the *Saturday Review*, he recorded, "The only link between literature and drama left to us in England at the present moment is the bill of the play," an incisive quip that revealed the essence of his involvement in the theater.

Wilde loved his first nights and was enchanted with his success as a dramatist. Offstage, many were the recipients of his witty asides—Sir Henry Irving among them. "Irving's legs are distinctly precious—but his left leg is a positive poem!"

Actresses were not Oscar's favorite people; if deserving, even the most distinguished were not exempt from his verbal admonishment, as one celebrated actress of the day had good cause to know. After a traumatic domestic life with her first husband she had remarried on the rebound to a man whom most of her friends regarded as a fool. Wilde was heard to comment, "She thought that because he was stupid he would be kindly when, of course, kindliness requires imagination and intellect."

If Wilde wasn't over-fond of many actresses, he was often less than deferential to actors of whom, as a breed, he held the view, "English actors act quite well, but they have the disconcerting habit of acting between the lines."

Fun was always a predominant force in Wilde's life, especially when his success in the theater was firmly established. With the sound of its London applause still echoing, *Lady Windermere's Fan* opened in New York. Awaiting the arrival of a cable which was to tell him of the success or failure of the play, the playwright paced up and down his room in an impatient mood. When a friend sought to assure him that all would be well, his face was said to have wrinkled with amusement as he exclaimed, "But this suspense is unbearable . . . I do hope it will last!"

... AND THAT WOMAN OF NO
IMPORTANCE

> *Wit is the sudden marriage of ideas which be-*
> *fore their union were not perceived to have*
> *any relation.*
>
> —Mark Twain
> *Notebook*, 1935

Having reached the heights with *Lady Windermere's Fan*, Wilde was determined to consolidate his commercial success. He began to write *A Woman of No Importance*. It was destined to confirm his genius.

On 19 April 1893, *A Woman of No Importance* opened at the Theatre Royal, Haymarket, London. If *Lady Windermere's Fan* had broken with theatrical convention—and shocked and delighted London—*A Woman of No Importance* was calculated to outdo its forerunner in its hedonistic wit. The play was rapturously received. The first-night audience was not content to greet the play with formal applause; the packed theater rose as one and demanded both sight and sound of the author. Wilde greeted his idolators from a box with his now-celebrated "author" speech: "Ladies and gentlemen, I regret to inform you that Mr. Oscar Wilde is not in the House!" upon which he was cheered to the echo.

After the final curtain, Oscar—glamorous as ever—was surrounded in the foyer by friends and sycophants. He was the recipient of bouquets, compliments, and effusive flattery from all except one first-nighter: The man handed the playwright an over-ripe cabbage and, in doing so, bowed deeply. Oscar smiled, "Thank you, my dear fellow. Every time I smell it, I shall be reminded of you!"

Despite the tumultous reception of A Woman of No Importance, Wilde still could not please the newspaper critics who this time accused him of "slow development of plot," "lack of action," "theatrical verbosity," and "an insufferable surfeit of paradoxical and epigrammatic dialogue." Again, their words had no effect on either the author or the box office, except that Wilde subsequently took up his pen wittily to lambast certain of the scribes in letters to newspapers.

In the eyes of his ever-growing legion of followers, the Master could do no wrong. America tried to lure him with fulsome praise and offers of crisp, green dollars. On the continent of Europe, his name was fast becoming legendary. Scarcely a day passed without French and other overseas papers carrying stories and pictures of him. Reporters recorded his every public utterance.

The celebrated actor-manager Herbert Beerbohm Tree (later knighted) came in for Wilde's verbal "punishment." While discussing with him the role of Lord Illingworth in A Woman of No Importance, Wilde held forth commandingly. "Before you can successfully impersonate the characters I have in mind, you must forget that you ever played Hamlet; you must forget that you ever played Falstaff; above all, you must forget that you ever played a Duke in that melodrama by Henry Arthur Jones. . . ." Tree replied that he would do his best. But Wilde was in his stride. "Indeed, I think that you had better forget that you ever acted at all!" Taken aback, Tree demanded to know why. "Because," said Wilde, "this witty aristrocrat whom you wish to assume in my play is quite unlike anyone who has ever been seen on a stage before. I will go further. He is like no-one who has existed before." "My God," exclaimed Tree, "he must be supernatural!" "Certainly," confirmed Wilde, "he is not natural. He is a figure of art. Indeed, if you can bear the truth, Herbert, he is myself!"

A *Woman of No Importance* had been written in London, Babbacombe, and Cromer where, between writing stints, Oscar played golf, at which he was appallingly bad—almost as bad as Tree who would, as often as not, drive off at the start of a game, lose sight of the ball, look at his watch, and say, "That's quite enough for one day!"—and leave the green. In this approach to the game, Oscar was the actor-manager's soul mate.

Wilde travelled to Glasgow to read his play to Tree, who was delighted with it. A contract was prepared at the Central Hotel and signed. Tree was full of enthusiasm for the project and was effusive in his compliments. The author was amusingly indifferent. "Plots," he said languorously, "are always tedious." He then admitted that he had taken the idea from *The Family Herald,* "which took it, wisely, from my novel, *The Picture of Dorian Gray.*"

"People," he added, "love a wicked aristocrat who seduces a virtuous girl, and they love a virtuous girl for being seduced by a wicked aristocrat. So that they may learn to appreciate what I like to give them, I have given them what they like. . . ."

Wilde and Tree were in many ways kindred beings. Both were generous (apart from Tree's tough bargaining powers and shrewd sense of business economics); both loved the good life. Tree had an almost worshipful appreciation of Wilde, except when it came to rehearsals. These, for *A Woman of No Importance*, started on 27 March 1893.

Theatrical legend has it that Tree ordered Wilde to stay away from rehearsals, but this is not borne out by Tree's half-brother, Max, who claimed the banning happened to playwright Henry Arthur Jones, not Wilde. Max told Hesketh Pearson that Herbert "delighted in Wilde's company" and retold the story, originally related by Oscar's son Vyvyan, that Tree and Wilde once met outside the theater. Tree, in frock coat sporting a red carnation, nonchalantly handled an elegant top hat with a crimson silk lining. "My dear Herbert," exclaimed Oscar, "what a charming hat lining." "My dear Oscar, do you really like it?" "I think it is perfection." "Then it is yours," and so saying, Tree ripped out the lining and handed it to Wilde with a mock bow, upon which he turned and walked into the theater.

In Tree, Wilde had a natural link with laughter. He had chivvied the actor-manager about Lord Illingworth being based on himself, and he teased him about his capacity as an actor to portray the part—of Wilde!—realistically. Oscar apparently met up with Squire Bancroft at London's Garrick Club. The Squire was later to divulge the dialogue that took place: "I'm told you've written the new Haymarket play?" "Say rather," corrected Wilde, "that the Haymarket has asked me for a play. . . ." "Hmm . . . I gather Tree is doing it?" "Alas, yes," affirmed Wilde. "But won't he be good in the role?" "Good? No." "But, surely, not bad?" "Bad? No." "Indifferent, what?" "No. Not indifferent." "Then what in God's name will he be?" "In the strictest confidence," confided Wilde, "and you promise not to repeat this?" "Not a word, I assure you." "Then I will whisper it in your deaf ear. Tree will be—we must face it manfully!—he will be Tree!"

The badinage seldom ceased between Wilde and Tree; it

was always good-humored and teasing. "You know. Herbert, I shall always regard you as my best critic," said Wilde. "But I have never criticized your plays, Oscar." "That's why!" rejoined the playwright with a dazzling smile.

Small wonder that Tree was universally liked in and out of the theatre. Even the taciturn, introspective Sir James Barrie said of him, "The magic of his personality brightened me every time I came near it, and the unworldliness of him was always attractive. He really was bigger than other people." And Oscar's assessment? "A charming fellow, and so clever. He models himself on me!"

By all accounts, Herbert Beerbohm Tree was supremely good in the role of Lord Illingworth, and while the production was enjoying its successful London run, Tree admitted that Illingworth was his favorite role.

Offstage, he would toss off Wilde's stage witticisms in the sophisticated style of Lord Illingworth to all and sundry. Wilde, who seldom missed a trick, was heard to comment, "Ah, every day, dear Herbert becomes *de plus en plus Oscarisé; it is a wonderful case of Nature imitating Art!"

It should be mentioned that Tree himself had a telling wit. During the run of the play, he encountered an actor who enthusiastically told him that he had been on the stage for forty-five years. Tree was alleged to have remarked, "Really, really! Almost a lifetime, eh? Any experience?" Wilde, when he heard this story, was said to have enjoyed it hugely. He may not have heard Tree's delightful comment when, upon being asked by an actor if life was really worth living, replied, "It depends on the liver!"

A Woman of No Importance gave rise in Act I to the memorable, ". . . the English country gentleman galloping after a fox—the unspeakable in full pursuit of the uneatable . . ." And Mrs. Allonby's line, "I delight in men over seventy; they always offer one the devotion of a lifetime!" She also remarked, when discussing 'the Ideal Man,' "He should always say much more than he means, and always mean much more than he says!"

The dialogue was stimulating and original—"A man who can dominate a London dinner-table can dominate the world. The future belongs to the dandy. It is the exquisites who are going to rule." Wilde dared, too, to poke fun at the Bible— "The Book of Life begins with a man and woman in a garden. It ends with Revelations." And theatregoers perceived the truth with the line, "I was influenced by my mother. Every man is when he is young . . ." A summary perhaps of Wilde's own youth?

At different times in his literary life he seemed to be preoccupied with sphinxes. He published his long poem "The Sphinx"—an even more lavish publication than his earlier "A House of Pomegranates"—while *A Woman Of No Importance* was playing to packed houses, in which he described women as "Sphinxes without Secrets." Later on, his story "The Sphinx Without a Secret" was published, no doubt inspired by the dialogue from the play, or perhaps it was just the mystical symbol of Eastern culture that captured his Muse?

Wilde would have been most unpopular had the era of the late nineteenth century boasted an active Women's Liberation movement. He certainly would have been a major target of attack for daring to opine, as he did, "I don't believe in women thinking too much. Women should think in moderation, as they should do all things in moderation"; and he was still preoccupied by women and original (and unoriginal!) sin. "What," he asked, "have women who have not sinned to do with me, or I with them? We do not understand each other."

Fred Terry, brother of Dame Ellen Terry, who played Gerald Arbuthnot in Wilde's original production of *A Woman of No Importance*, was not in total sympathy with the author's conception of the role. Joining up with his wife, Julia Neilson, who played Hester Worsley, and who was also not entirely happy with her role, the two were invited to lunch by Wilde to discuss their objections. Terry happened to be an avid admirer of Charles Dickens, so it was not surprising that the talk soon turned to the author of *Great Expectations et al.*

Wilde proceeded to deliver a long and eulogistic assessment of the talents of the great Victorian author. Terry, not unnaturally, warmed to Wilde's words. After their animated discussion on Dickens had ended, precious little time predictably was left for discussion of Wilde's own play. But the playwright, with his usual charm and persuasion, quickly gained Terry's full approval to his interpretative ideas for the role. Julia Neilson, too, concurred with the author's thoughts about her part and its interpretation. The party rose from the table. Terry shook Wilde's hand warmly, commenting, "My dear Oscar, it has been a great pleasure to me to discover another who shares my enthusiasm for Charles Dickens. Thank you." Wilde smiled intriguingly. "My dear boy," he drawled, "I must now tell you that I've never read a word of Dickens in my life!" The luncheon party ended in excellent humor. Wilde had won the day, albeit not without deceit. He had read most of Dickens and could not stand him!

Actors and actresses mouthed his words in theaters everywhere—and they were always lines that were unmistakably Wilde, usually mounted on one or more of his aphoristic hobby horses. "Every woman," he wrote, "is a rebel, and usually in wild revolt against herself." He grew more intrepid in extending this theme as *A Woman of No Importance* grew in box office stature: "The history of women is the history of the worst form of tyranny the world has ever known. The tyranny of the weak over the strong. It is the only tyranny that lasts!" Then, unexpectedly, he would lay an epicurean bait, and hold forth with "After a good dinner one can forgive anybody, even one's own relations!" and go on to explain that "The only difference between the saint and the sinner is that every saint has a past, and every sinner a future!"

Perhaps Wilde was right when he had Lord Illingworth lament, "All thought is immoral. Its very essence is destruction. If you think of anything, you kill it. Nothing survives being thought of."

He had previously espoused the view that "Fathers should neither be seen nor heard," which, he claimed was "the only proper basis for family life."

There is little doubt that Wilde genuinely liked children. Was he not on record as having said, "The best way to make children is to make them happy"? And he had previously penned, "The pleasure to me was being with those who are young, bright, happy, careless and free. I do not like the sensible and I do not like the old." Again emerges the omnipresent preoccupation with youth and age. "The young are always ready to give those who are older than themselves the full benefit of their inexperience."

Wilde had declared with satirical accuracy, "A bishop keeps on saying at the age of eighty what he was told to say when he was a boy of eighteen," and he had, too, nostalgically and not without irony, again recalled his own youth. "When I was young I used to think that money was the most important thing in life; now that I am old, I know it!"

In *A Woman of No Importance,* he returned to his theme. "Children begin by loving their parents. After a time they judge them. Rarely, if ever, do they forgive them!"

This logic in the play might be deemed near faultless: "When a man is old enough to do wrong, he should be old enough to do right also."

We might question his advice (but never his wit) on how to get one's fingers burned: "The one advantage of playing with fire is that one never gets even singed. It is the people who don't know how to play with it who get burned up."

Again in the play, he had one of his characters spout, "Everything you have said today seems to me excessively immoral. It has been interesting listening to you!"

In so much of Wilde's writing, he suddenly and disconcertingly displays through the words of his characters an almost baffling and uncharacteristic tenderness, as in A *Woman of No Importance*, when he says, "The sick do not ask if the hand that smoothes their pillow is pure, nor the dying care if the lips that touch their brow have known the kiss of sin." Was this Wilde the poet emerging? It was certainly Wilde the wit and cynic who expressed the view that "I don't think there is a woman in the world who would not be a little flattered if one made love to her. It is that which makes women so irrisistibly adorable!" In similar vein, he held the controversial opinion that "Plain women are always jealous of their husbands. Beautiful women never have time. They are always so occupied in being jealous of other people's husbands!"

On the theme of lack of beauty in women, he expounded, "I don't mind plain women being Puritans. It is the only excuse they have for being plain!" He did, however, concede, "The happiness of a married man depends on the people he has not married!"

Wilde could—and occasionally did—descend to music-hall type humor. For example, in A *Woman of No Importance*, Mrs. Allonby says, "My husband is a sort of promissory note; I'm tired of meeting him!" But wisdom takes flight when one of his characters opines, "Nothing spoils a romance so much as a sense of humour in a woman—or the want of it in a man!"

Let's try him on the sensitive subject of "first love": "Men always want to be a woman's first love. That is their clumsy vanity. Women have a more subtle instinct about things. What they like is to be a man's last romance!"

Wilde's perception of life was remarkable. Listen: "A kiss may ruin a human life. . . ." In that single truism is the essence of a million past and present life-dramas, and who but Wilde could have considered its inclusion in a play of high comedy like *A Woman of No Importance?*

His sheer audacity was the highlight of his writing, particularly his writings for the theatre. Here is another, equally short example: "Who, being loved, is poor?"—a skeletal economy of words projecting a world of unarguable logic. Another axiom: "Men are horribly tedious when they are good husbands, and abominably conceited when they are not!"

Hear the Master again on the wiles of women: "All men are married women's property. That is the only true definition of what married women's property really is!"

The "logic" of others was relatively unimportant. Came the challenge, and within seconds there followed the unarguable Wildean answer: "Music makes one feel so romantic—at least it always gets on one's nerves; which is the same thing nowadays. . . ."

On the social front, too, he led the field: "To have been well brought up is a great drawback nowadays. It shuts one out from so much!"

Another cryptic comment: "Moods don't last. It is their chief charm!"

He once said to James McNeill Whistler, after a Whistler witticism, "I wish I'd said that!" If the wish be father to the thought, he had need to emulate no one when he could write, as he did, "Moderation is a fatal thing. In Life as in Art, nothing succeeds like excess!"—an axiom still laughingly quoted as often today as when *A Woman of No Importance* enjoyed its first London run not far short of a hundred years ago.

Even today's politicians might do well to heed Wilde's theatrical tenet, "Discontent is the first step in the progress of a man or a nation." Trade unionists might be prepared to give hearty applause to *that* utterance.

"Life," said Oscar in the play, "is simply a *mauvais quart d'heure*, made up of exquisite moments . . . ," a thought perhaps a little too exquisite for most of us who have to be concerned with the daily grind. But no matter, Oscar is ever ready to change his mood of the moment. "The world," he claimed, "has been made by fools that wise men should live in it." He might well have added that wise men have frequently been made wise by fools.

There must be many who would share his belief that *"The Peerage* is the one book a young man-about-town should know thoroughly and it is the best thing in fiction the English have ever done." And, "Englishwomen," he considered, "conceal their feelings till after they are married. They show them then"—a remark that even today is likely to gain immediate worldwide male chauvinistic support!

You may, perhaps, prefer Lady Stutfield's laconic line, "The secret of life is to appreciate the pleasure of being terribly, terribly deceived," and his earlier point on the peerage is well and truly underlined in Act III of *A Woman of No Importance:* "If a man is a gentleman, he knows quite well enough: and if he is not a gentleman whatever he knows is bad for him!"

Wilde also wistfully claimed "to adore simple pleasures; they are," he explained, "the last refuge of the complex!" He had, too, a few words on the art of conversation. "Clever people never listen, and stupid people never talk."

Wilde bared another essential truth with this sally: "The secret of life is never to have an emotion that is unbecoming," but how inconvenient for mere mortals!

In Act I, an effective enough truism was, "One should never trust a woman who tells one her real age. A woman who would tell one that, would tell one anything!"; while Act III of the play, swaying with towering truths, threw up this classic: "When one is in love one begins to deceive oneself. And one ends up deceiving others."

In *A Woman of No Importance* he couldn't resist a jab at the British Establishment.

Kelvil: May I ask, Lord Illingworth, if you regard the House of Lords as a better institution than the House of Commons?

Illingworth: A much better institution, of course. We in the House of Lords are never in touch with public opinion. That makes us a civilised body!

Oscar's son Vyvyan has since written that to Oscar "words were beautiful baubles with which to play and build, as a child plays with coloured bricks." In 1894, Oscar Wilde studiously played long and hard with his "beautiful baubles." In that year, he wrote his last two plays, the incomparably comic *An Ideal Husband* and the happy and hilarious *The Importance of Being Earnest.*

THE "REGENT STREET ROYALIST"

Where is Oscar,
Where is Bosie,
Have I seen that man before?
And the old one in the corner,
Is it really Wratislaw?
(Scent of tutti-frutti sen-sen
And cheeroots upon the floor)
> —Extract from a poem scribbled in Café Royal autograph book, circa 1965, by John Betjeman, on seeing octogenarian Arthur Symons, an old Café habitué, enter the restaurant as Betjeman was leaving

The most Bohemian habitat in London's West End before, during, and to a great extent after Oscar Wilde's reign as the darling of the capital's social and artistic set, was Regent Street's Café Royal. Here, in the Domino Room with its marble-topped tables, the famous, the notorious, the affluent, and the penurious foregathered daily. It mattered not if you were hard up; the unforgiving minute could always be stretched to three or four hours over a coffee or a glass of *vin ordinaire*, although, for those who could afford fine wines, Frank Harris was later to record that "Even in 1884-5 the Café Royal had the best cellar in the world. Fifteen years later it was the best ever seen on earth."

Before and at the height of his fame, Wilde was a Café habitué. The ornate gilded mirrors reflected a formidable procession of artistic giants of the stature of Fritz Kreisler, American-born artist James McNeill Whistler (who used to sign his bills with a butterfly mark), D. H. Lawrence, Toulouse-Lautrec, Jacob Epstein, the even more bizarre and erotic Aleister Crowley, the arrogant young politician Winston Churchill, Paul Verlaine, Ireland's W. B. Yeats, the eclectic Ronald Firbank, Ernest "Cynara" Dowson, T. W. H. Crosland, Max Beerbohm, and painters like Alfred Munnings (later to be knighted), C. W. Nevinson, Laura Knight (later to become Dame), and W. R. Sickert, as well as writers like Hugh Walpole (who was also to achieve a knighthood), Rupert Brooke's close friend Sir Edward Marsh, and, later still, T. S. Eliot, Aldous Huxley, *et al.* Above the formidable assemblage of his time towered the powerful, flamboyant figure of Oscar Wilde, green carnation in his buttonhole, surrounded by friends, enemies, and acolytes.

The Café attracted not only epicures, gourmets, poets, writers, artists, painters, and musicians, but many other intellectuals who, too, found the informal clublike atmosphere both stimulating and agreeable. Epstein—later Sir Jacob—would doodle on the marble-topped tables, as would Augustus John and Sickert. On one occasion, Auguste Rodin, given a subscription dinner by his English admirers, painted a rural scene over the entire top of one of the tables.

What the Mermaid Tavern was to the Elizabethans, Wills's London Coffee House to the Augustans, and The Cock to the mid-Victorians, the Café Royal was to the late Victorians—especially Oscar Wilde. He used many restaurants, but this was his favourite haunt, celebrated for its "sounds of revelry by night"—so celebrated, in fact, that it boasted the singular and cryptic telegraphic address, "Restaurant, London."

During and since those days it has figured prominently in plays, films, memoirs, and has been immortalized in poems and novels, among them Sir Arthur Conan Doyle's *The Il-*

lustrious Client. D. H. Lawrence disguised it as the "Café Pompadour" in his *Women In Love.* Arnold Bennett, Somerset Maugham, G. K. Chesterton, and Evelyn Waugh named it or disguised it in published tales; later, Graham Greene, Osbert Sitwell, and many others also immortalized it in print; of recent vintage, John Wyndham's vegetable monsters persuaded a bemused mob to "take it over" in his terrifying film *The Day of the Triffids.* In 1979, much of the action of the Robert Morley film *Too Many Cooks* was filmed there.

Are there left today any who can recall the Café in the late nineties? Alas, no. But the venerable author Beverley Nichols (no relation to the Café's founder, Daniel Nichols), talked of the Café, as it was after the turn of the century:

> The very first person with whom I ever went to the Café Royal when I was a very young undergraduate was the celebrated Lord Alfred Douglas. I insisted that we should lunch at the same table where he had last lunched with Oscar Wilde. . . .

> If you ask me why I was going about with Lord Alfred Douglas at that time, it's because I was hoping to sue him for libel, but he very wisely got away with lunch instead. . . .

> You know, people really were at their best, I think—perhaps a little larger than life, than themselves, when they went to the Café Royal.

> Sir Thomas Beecham, quite a young man, would conduct the soufflé with a fork, and you'd have all sorts of marvellous parties. Well, of course, you have parties develop from cafés today, but these at the Café Royal seemed to me to have a very particular glamour. It was just after Oscar Wilde's heyday, but I remember Tallulah Bankhead, who was very, very beautiful in those days, arrived there and we all gathered round her and took her off to a party at my shack. We found a red carpet on the way and somehow it ended up with Tallulah being dragged through the streets in the direction of the House of Commons and my flat on a red carpet. . . .

A favorite Café Royal character of Wilde's was the tall, gaunt, white-faced Yorkshireman, T. W. H. Crosland who, realizing that he looked like an undertaker, would present those introduced to him with a grubby, black-edged visiting card inscribed with his name and "occupation"—Jobbing Poet, Funerals Attended!

Crosland virtually lived in the Domino Room, spending his time there arguing about poetry and, imbibing in sequence, lager, sloe gin, whiskey and soda, brandy, hock, burgundy, and champagne. Most of this inebriating rota was consumed on the generosity of his friends, notably Wilde, for Crosland seldom had any money. He had an obsessive passion for riding in cabs—and much of what he did earn found its way into the pockets of cab drivers. He would frequently keep a cab waiting for him outside the Café all night while he imbibed and argued with eccentric glee until the first hesitant light of morning.

Crosland's speciality was invective: He assumed an air of perpetual rudeness to others. He wrote a highly controversial attack upon the English called *The Egregious English*, and most of his other books followed the same pattern—*The Unspeakable Scot, Taffy Was A Welshman, The Abounding American, A Fine Old Hebrew Gentleman*, and even one called *The Unspeakable Crosland*, an anonymous attack on himself! He was later to figure in a contumacious literary episode as a co-author with Lord Alfred Douglas.

But let us return to Oscar and the Café. When Wilde first frequented the Domino Room at the Café Royal, James McNeill Whistler, twenty years his senior, was the uncrowned king of the "royalists of Regent Street"; Wilde, young, zestful, ambitious, paid Whistler due deference, for was it not Whistler who had defined, "Wit is the power to say what everybody else would like to have said, if they had happened to think of it"? A man after Oscar's own heart!

The two became uneasy companions, ate mainly chops and vegetables at the Café, and drank an inexpensive but excellent claret that Whistler himself had pounced on during a nocturnal foray in the Café's cellars far under the Regent Street pavements. It has accurately been said that their friendship was not of enduring quality. Wilde wrote of Whistler in a letter to *World*, "With our James, vulgarity begins at home, and should be allowed to stay there."

Both intellectually brilliant, they were, to some extent, natural rivals for the domination of the artistic clique of the Café. Had not legend whispered to Wilde the Whistler story of a Bostonian grande dame who had questioned the painter about his origins? Whistler had said that he had made his debut into the world "in a hick town somewhere in Massachusetts." "Why, Mr. Whistler," the lady cried in haughty reproof, "what on earth possessed you to be born in a place like that?" "The explanation, Madam," Whistler had replied, "was because I wished to be near my mother!"

The story was much to Wilde's liking, as was the anecdote concerning Whistler's commission to paint an inordinately ugly male patron. The work completed, artist and subject contemplated the finished portrait. "I fear," observed the ugly male, "one can hardly call this a great work of art." "Perhaps not," replied Whistler, "but then you can hardly call yourself a classic work of Nature!"

And Wilde learned of Whistler's reply to a portly woman who loudly proclaimed that she knew of only two really supreme painters in the world. "And who are they?" she was asked by "Jimmy" Whistler. "Whistler and Velásquez," came the quick reply, to which Whistler was reputed to have observed, "Why drag in Valasquez?"

Wilde had sat in Whistler's company at the Café when another voluble female had interrupted the talk to ask Whistler whether he considered genius to be hereditary. Whistler turned slowly, regarded the woman with a distant, glassy stare, and replied, "I regret, Madam, I cannot tell you. Heaven has granted me no offspring!"

Whistler, with Frank Miles and others, would frequently eat at Wilde's home. Edward W. Bok has told how he was asked to join them at breakfast at Oscar's house:

> I noticed as I sat down that next to me, at my left, had been placed a man instead of the usual rotation. I turned to my left to find my neighbour had pushed his chair back from the table about three feet, and buried his chin in his shirt-bosom and was reaching forth for his eatables, and practically eating them from his lap, his cup resting on his knee.

> There was something familiar about the features of my neighbour who was eating in the most grotesque fashion I ever saw, and yet I couldn't place him. I looked for his place-card, but I could see none. So I shoved back my chair and tried to engage him in conversation. But I was not rewarded by even a glance.

> When I asked a question I received either no answer at all or a grunt. After a few heroic efforts, I gave up the struggle. At the close of the breakfast, I asked Wilde:—Who in the world was that chap on my left?

> I know, returned Wilde, I saw your valiant struggle! He gets that way once in a while, and this morning happened to be one of those whiles. That was my American friend, Whistler!

This, then, was Oscar's premier Café rival.

About this time, an English newspaper printed the following tidbit of gossip: "James McNeill Whistler and Oscar Wilde were seen yesterday at Brighton, talking as usual about themselves. . . ." Whistler sent the paragraph to Wilde with a note saying, "I wish these reporters would be accurate. If you remember, Oscar, we were talking about me!"

Showing Whistler a poem he had written that morning,

Oscar sought the painter's opinion. Whistler stared at the sheet of paper for some time, gaining a telling effect. Then, with a deliberate gesture, he handed the wafer-thin sheet back to Oscar, pronouncing solemnly, "Your poem is worth its weight in gold!" It is said that Wilde never forgave him, and then and there determined to unseat the king from his Bohemian throne.

He eventually took over from Whistler and created his own salon at the Café. His admirers were well fed and watered; Wilde was both a gourmet and a gourmand. Lord Alfred Douglas said he would back Wilde to eat the head off a brewer's drayman three times a day; but in spite of the quantity of food and drink consumed, Oscar was also very particular about quality.

Choosing wine to go with the food was to Wilde an exacting and exotic ritual, to be performed on special occasions only, with gravity and reverence. The chef was summoned and given detailed instructions about each course; the choice of wines was lovingly discussed with the sommelier. He was a particular devotee of the *Cliquot vin rose* and insisted (with not unpardonable color accuracy) in calling white wine "yellow." He was particularly partial to hock mixed with seltzer.

Wilde attracted his vast following because he was the supreme conversationalist of his age. Whatever disputes there may have been about his place in literature—and these grew fewer with the years—his standing as a wit remained unimpaired. Only a few demurred, among them the painter Walter Sickert, who chided, "It was easy to get the laughs if you carried your own claque about."

But the claque still applauded, and many brilliant and notorious names paid idolatrous court at Oscar's Café table. These included the sober brilliance of Rothenstein, occasionally the ascetic fire of Shaw, frequently the doomed glitter of Beardsley, and, invariably, the bombast and shrewdness of Frank

Harris. There were many who would sit nearby for long periods in the expectance of overhearing the odd epigram of Wildean aphorism. They were seldom disappointed.

As far as the Café management was concerned, Wilde was an asset *in excelsis:* His mere presence brought the customers flocking into the Domino Room.

It has been said that for Oscar "the Café Royal was not merely a restaurant, nor yet a Club." It was a court—*his* court, the Court of Oscar Wilde. And now, preening majestically even above Whistler, he was his own official Court Jester.

MARRIAGE, EDITORSHIP,
AND FOUR BOOKS

What is a woman? Only one of Nature's
agreeable blunders.
                              —HANNAH COWLEY (1743-1809)

This, then, was the leisure world of Oscar Wilde, surrounded by saints, sinners, sycophants, and sophistry. The
tenuous friendship between Wilde and Whistler finally ended
when Whistler gave a major public lecture which Wilde attended. Wilde wrote a lengthy review of it in the *Pall Mall
Gazette* of 21 February 1885; it was devastating in its debunk-
ing originality. "The scene," recorded Wilde, "was in every
way delightful. [Whistler] stood there, a miniature Mephi-
stopheles, mocking the majority! He was like a brilliant
surgeon lecturing to a class composed of subjects destined ulti-
mately for dissection, and solemnly assuring them how valu-
able to science their maladies were and how absolutely
uninteresting the slightest symptoms of health on their part
would be." He concluded, "That Mr. Whistler is indeed one

of the greatest masters of painting, is my opinion. And I may add that with this opinion Mr. Whistler himself entirely concurs. . . ."

Whistler, who, like Shaw, claimed that much of Wilde's writing was derivative, was livid. Although he fought back in a torrid exchange of public letters, he never spoke to Wilde again.

Wilde, having finished his series of lectures in England and Scotland, was becoming slightly bored by his public "image." He felt a need for more secure roots and, soon afterwards, announced his engagement to Constance Mary Lloyd, an Irish barrister's daughter who, with members of her family, had met him both in Ireland and in London.

Before Constance, Oscar had undergone the sensitive experience of "first love" in Dublin with an enchanting Irish girl, Florence Balcombe, who eventually married Bram Stoker, author of *Dracula.*

It was on a visit to Dublin that Oscar first proposed marriage to Constance Lloyd. They eventually became betrothed at St. James's Church, Paddington, London, on 29 May 1884. After honeymooning in Paris, the two returned to take up temporary residence in Oscar's rooms in Charles Street, Mayfair, while awaiting the redecoration of a house they had taken at 16 Tite Street.

The Wildes, surrounded by lovely pictures, drawings, books, and pieces of exquisite sculpture, established their London salon. They were soon entertaining the celebrated from all walks of life: actors and actresses, including Bernhardt and Langtry, painters, poets, politicians, editors, impresarios, and even the American scribe-cum-unofficial-diplomat Mark Twain on his frequent visits to London.

Constance, an accomplished pianist and a somewhat timorous writer, had a small allowance from her family. But living at such a rate of assumed affluence was like living in a dream world. Here was Oscar, conversationalist *extraordinaire*, heavily publicized wit and raconteur, a genius with words, vilified, lampooned, and caricatured, hated, envied, admired—a bon vivant, with apparently the world at his feet. Yet in reality he was an almost penniless poet and writer.

It says much for Constance, with whom he was very much in love and on whom he showered variegated and expensive benedictions of that love, that she shared the oppressive load of his acute money worries with a deep, affectionate concern. Happily, the marriage was blessed by the birth of two sons, Cyril and Vyvyan.

It was at this period that Oscar's writing fortunes took a turn for the better; this was the period of his provocative contributions to Frank Harris's *Pall Mall Gazette* and critiques for the *Dramatic Review*. Later, in 1887, he was to become editor of *The Lady's World*, a monthly magazine that subsequently, much enlarged and more expensively produced, became *The Woman's World*. To the columns of his "new toy" he attracted the greatest names in literature and the arts: Whitman, Pater, Yeats, Ouida, Edith Nesbit—they virtually queued up in support of the Irish literary genius and his magazine. But after a couple of years, Oscar became "devilishly bored" with the routine of operating and administering a London editorial office and resigned.

In his spare time during his two years as editor, he had written poetry, essays, and short stories, including "The Canterville Ghost" and "Lord Arthur Savile's Crime." A number of these short stories were later assembled into one volume and published as *Lord Arthur Savile's Crime and Other Stories*.

Leaving the magazine, he turned his time to good account, applied himself assiduously once more, and published four books: *The House of Pomegranates*, the *Lord Arthur* volume, *The Picture of Dorian Gray* (a novel originally printed in a shorter version in *Lippincott's Monthly*), and a book of four masterly essays, "The Decay of Lying," "Pen, Pencil and Poison, "The Critic as Artist," and "The Truth of Masks," under the title *Intentions*. When this work appeared, it created a torrent of adulatory and adverse criticism. The essays, serious in their philosophical approach, nevertheless contained vintage Wildean wit which irritated the envious and delighted his devotees. "One is tempted," he wrote, "to define man as a rational animal who always loses his temper when he is called upon to act in accordance with the dictates of reason." This was Wilde at his philosophical best.

In "The Decay of Lying," said by many to be his best work, he upbraided George Meredith in these words: "His style is chaos, illumined by flashes of lightning. As a writer, he has mastered everything but language."

Irreverence was his "tribute" to a distinguished Lake poet: "Wordsworth went to the lakes, but he was never a Lake poet. He found in stones the sermons he had already hidden there."

As for America's venerated Henry James, Wilde observed, ". . . [he] writes fiction as if it were a painful duty. . . ."

Wilde considered, too, that "Society sooner or later must return to its lost leader, the cultured and fascinating liar"; and, warming to his theme, he postulated, "People have a careless way of talking about a 'born liar' just as they talk about a 'born poet.' Lying and poetry are arts—arts, as Plato saw—not unconnected with each other, and they require the most careful study, the most interesting devotion. . . . After all," he asked, "what is a fine lie? Simply that which is its own evidence!" He went on to lambast the reader, this time on the theme of George Washington's lie and the imperishable cherry tree.

Was there an autobiographical echo in his recently completed *The Picture of Dorian Gray*, with his assertion that

"The only portraits in which one believes are portraits where there is very little of the sitter and a very great deal of the artist"?

His words on art and artists took on an even more devastating cutting edge when he held that "Most of our modern portrait painters are doomed to oblivion. They never paint what they see. They paint what the public sees, and the public never sees anything."

As for the processes of thinking, Wilde rose to heady heights:

Thinking is the most unhealthy thing in the world, and people die of it just as they die of any other disease. Fortunately, in England, at any rate, thought is not catching. Our splendid physique as a people is entirely due to our national stupidity. . . .

Novelists were not exempt. He held,

The only real people are the people who never existed and if a novelist is base enough to go to life for his personages he should at least pretend that they are creations and not boast of them as copies.

Literature always anticipates life. It does not copy it, but moulds it to its purpose. The nineteenth-century as we know it, is largely an invention of Balzac!

And, he reminded his readers, "The ancient historians gave us delightful fiction in the form of fact; the modern novelist presents us with dull facts under the guise of fiction"; but he *was* ready to concede, "I quite admit that modern novels have many good points. All I insist on is that, as a class, they are quite unreadable!"

The popular romantic scene was suspect, too: "At twilight nature becomes a wonderfully suggestive effect, and is not without loveliness, though perhaps its chief use is to illustrate quotations from the poets."

In "The Decay of Lying," he was back on a familiar platform: "The proper school to learn art is not Life but Art."

The established Church of England received this treatment: "The growth of common sense in the English Church is a thing very much to be regretted. It is really a degrading concession to a low form of reality," and similar hubris emerged on the topic of education: "Everybody who is incapable of learning has taken to teaching." Then he added, "That is really what our enthusiasm for education has come to."

Moreover, he was not prepared to allow painters any leeway in his earlier protestations about their professional pursuits. "No great artist," he wrote with virulent vigor, "ever sees things as they really are," underlining his already expressed thought, "if he did he would cease to be an artist!"

He had little time for the then popular "sky-scapes," the still, romantic, painted representations of evening over the river, dreamy sunsets and the like. He argued,

Nobody of any real culture ever talks about the beauty of a sunset. Sunsets are quite old-fashioned. They belong to the time when Turner was the last note in art. To admire them is a distinct sign of provincialism. Yesterday evening, Mrs. Arundel insisted on my going to the window and looking at the "glorious sky," as she called it. Of course, I had to look at it. She is one of those absurdly pretty Philistines to whom one can deny nothing. . . .
And what was it? It was simply a very second-rate Turner, a Turner of bad period, with all the painter's worst faults exaggerated and over-emphasized.

This from "The Decay of Lying."

What might we expect from the contemptuous "Pen, Pencil and Poison"? In essence, this was a short, biographical pen-portrait of Thomas Griffiths Wainewright, the Victorian forger and murderer. Listen: "The first step in aesthetic criticism is to realise one's own impressions." Before the applause abated, he was back on his pet subject of masks: "Man is least himself when he talks in his own person. Give him a mask and he will tell you the truth." And, "A mask tells us more than a face."

It was, too, a frolicsome *divertissement* to consider his view that "All beautiful things belong to the same age," largely depending, one supposes, on the age in which you happened to live.

The subject of crime, suggested by the "Poison" of his title, brought him to Wainewright and philosophic mood: "Crime in England is rarely the result of sin. It is nearly always the result of starvation." Well said, for a sophisticate and gourmet!

Good and evil is an ever-recurring Wildean theme, as with "Society often forgives the criminal; it never forgives the dreamer."

Amusingly, if not unexpectedly, he seemed to take sides with the ex-journalist Wainewright. For *who* could argue with Wilde's witty view that "The fact of a man being a poisoner is nothing against his prose"?

Wilde's third essay in *Intentions*, "The Critic as Artist," was originally subtitled "With Some Remarks Upon the Importance of Doing Nothing"—again that word "importance." As Vyvyan, his son, observed,

> It is curious how the word seems to run through his works; it occurs in the titles of two of his plays, is constantly cropping up in his essays; it is almost as if the word held a strange sonorousness for him and that he liked to roll it, if not round his tongue, then round his mind. . . .

Wilde shared similar views with most published writers, exhibitors, artists, and professional performers on the subject of critics. He did not approve of them and frequently took them to task. In his disquisition on "The Critic as Artist," he analyzes critics and criticism, principally on a historical basis. He was equally astringent on the stability of society: "The security of society lies in custom and unconscious instinct, and the basis of stability of society, as a healthy organism, is the complete absence of any intelligence amongst its members." And not unfamiliar is the belief that "If we live long enough to see the results of our actions it may be those who call themselves good would be sickened with a dull remorse, and those whom the world calls evil stirred by a noble joy."

The conventional Irish intellectual on the subject of England is usually predictable; not so with Wilde. "England will never be civilised until she has added Utopia to her dominions," he admonished, adding, "The real weakness of England lies, not in incomplete armaments or unfortified coasts, not in the poverty that creeps through sunless lanes, or the drunkenness that brawls in loathsome courts, but simply in the fact that her ideals are emotional and not intellectual." Well, that's a show-stopper!

In spite of his dislike of the critics, he sometimes edged over to their aisle. "I am always amused by the silly vanity of those writers and artists of our day who seem to imagine that the primary function of the critic is to chatter about their second-rate work." He followed this by hitting out with precision and predictability at art critics in "The English Renaissance of Art:" "The first duty of an art critic is to hold his tongue at all times, and upon all subjects." It is obvious that so-called modern art in late Victorian times was as provocative as it is today. In Wilde's opinion, "The best that one can say of most modern creative art is that it is just a little less vulgar than reality." And he wasn't finished yet.

Modern pictures are, no doubt, delightful to look at. At least, some of them are. But they are quite impossible to live with; they are too clever, too assertive, too intellectual. Their meaning is too obvious, and their method too clearly defined. One exhausts what they have to say in a very short time, and then they become as tedious as one's relations.

He further considered that "Emotion for the sake of emotion is the aim of Art, and emotion for the sake of action is the aim of Life."

Most of the time it seemed that there was positively no pleasing him. Take journalism. "Journalism," he lambasted, "is unreadable, and literature is not read." And further,

> Journalists record only what happens. What does it matter what happens? It is only the abiding things that are interesting, not the horrid incidents of everyday life. Creation for the joy of creation is the aim of the artist, and that is why the artist is a more divine type than the saint. . . .

But Wilde had, himself, been a journalist and was close to the truth in his pronouncement that "The only thing that the artist cannot see is the obvious. The only thing the public can see is the obvious. The result is the criticism of the journalist." And, this time, on poetry, "All bad poetry springs from genuine feeling. To be natural is to be obvious, and to be obvious is to be inartistic."

He could also be biting about writers and writing. "Anybody can write a three-volume novel," he claimed, "it merely requires a complete ignorance of both life and literature"; and what about great Men and history's Heroes? "Formerly we used to canonise our heroes. The modern method is to vulgarise them. Cheap editions of great books may be delightful, but cheap editions of great men are absolutely detestable."

In "The Critic as Artist" he hints of profundity—but a frivolity inevitably intrudes: "The tears that we shed at a play are a type of the exquisite sterile emotions that it is the function of Art to awaken. We weep but we are not wounded. We grieve but our grief is not bitter." But should our grief be bitter? Wilde's answer was perhaps inherent in the same essay. "It is because Humanity has never known where it is going that it has been able to find its way." Or perhaps it all comes down to education? He claimed that "Education is an admirable thing, but it is well to remember from time to time that nothing that is worth knowing can be taught"! Well, that's education coolly dispatched out of the classroom window. Let's try him on Expression: "Find expression for a sorrow, and it will become dear to you. Find expression for a joy, and you intensify its ecstasy."

On history he was brief and to the point: "The one duty we owe to history is to rewrite it." Glib, perhaps, but somewhat qualified by his later declaration, "It is so much more difficult to talk about a thing than to do it. In the sphere of actual life, that is, of course, obvious. Anybody can make history. Only a great man can write it." One wonders what he would have said had he lived in the later Churchillian age? Did he, with his acute perception, see such an age on the horizon of time?

"When we have fully discovered the scientific laws that govern Life, we shall realize that the one person who has more illusions than the dreamer is the man of action."

Wilde, ever searching for effect, always knew a good line when he wrote one!

MASKS AND MAN

An aphorism is like a bee, fully burdened with
gold, but with a sting attached.
—CARMEN SYLVA (1843-1916)

Wilde was frequently accused of transferring paradoxes and aphorisms from salon conversation into his published or performed works. He was also accused by Whistler and Frank Harris of plagiarism. Whatever the truth, he certainly believed in revamping a telling line or phrase, as with, "Oh, don't say that you agree with me. When people agree with me I always feel I must be wrong," which the perceptive playgoer or reader will recognize from Act II of *Lady Windermere's Fan*. It crops up again in Part Two of "The Critic as Artist." But is it not the type of delicious wit that stands repetition?

If the heart of the popular biographer beats with any sort of sensitivity, he might well ponder the Master's allegorical reproach, "Every great man nowadays has his disciple, and it is always Judas who writes the biography." And what of the insanity of war? "As long as war is regarded as wicked, it will always have its fascinations. When it is looked upon as vulgar, it will cease to be popular."

There was always room for Wilde's tongue to be tucked into his ample cheek, especially if the subject of sincerity was in question. His comment on this is directed at lover and lackey, sycophant and cynic—whomsoever you will: "A little sincerity is a dangerous thing, and a great deal of it is absolutely fatal!"

His essay "The Truth of Masks," subtitled "A Note on Illusion," concerns the individual and the masks he assumes in the pursuit of everyday living. It also deals with the complexities of the theater, the world of make-believe, the mastery of costume, color, and theatrical performance—and, at some length, with Shakespeare and his Art. It is obvious that to Wilde the theater and its imagery afforded him much fascination.

[To the illusionist] the deformed figure of Richard was of as much value as Juliet's loveliness; he sets the serge of the radical beside the silks of the lord, and sees the stage effects to be got from each; he has as much delight in Caliban as he has in Ariel, in rags as he has in cloth of gold, and recognizes the artistic beauty of ugliness. . . .

The "recognition of the artistic beauty of ugliness" was something that Wilde normally refused to acknowledge; his writings elsewhere betray his total revulsion to ugliness in any shape or form, especially the human form.

There's this gem, too, from "The Truth of Masks."

In criticizing the importance given to money in *La Comédie Humaine,* Théophile Gautier says that Balzac may claim to have invented a new hero in fiction, *les Néros Métallique.* Of Shakespeare it may be said he was the first to see the dramatic value of doublets, and that a climax may depend on a crinoline. . . .

He certainly warmly endorsed his own axiom, "The stage is not merely the meeting-place of all the Arts, but is also the return of Art to Life." He held, too, that "Archeology is only really delightful when transfused into some form of Art."

There was a literary controversy involving Keats, *Lempriere's Dictionary,* and Professor Max Muller's treatment of "semantic mythology" as "a disease of language." Quipped Wilde, "Better *Endymion* than any theory, however sound—or unsound—of an epidemic among adjectives!" Moreover, he revealed in the same essay that "There is hardly a single title in the Upper House [of Lords] with the exception, of course, of the uninteresting titles assumed by the law Lords, which does not appear in Shakespeare along with many details of family history, creditable and discreditable. . . ." He went on to applaud the Bard with even more enthusiasm: "Indeed, if it be really necessary that the School Board ° children should know about the Wars of the Roses, they could learn their lessons just as well out of Shakespeare as out of shilling primers . . . and far more pleasurably!"

He was, too, a ready critic of the modern-dress theatrical productions of his time. "As a rule, the hero is smothered in bric-à-brac and palm trees, lost in the gilded abyss of Louis Quatorze furniture, or reduced into a mere midget in the midst of marqueterie. . . ." Such pungent alliteration is Wilde at his most amusing. He's equally entertaining on "the Facts of Art." "These," he claimed, "are diverse, but the essence of artistic effort is unity. Monarchy, Anarchy, and Republicanism may be content for the government of nations, but a theater should be in the power of a cultured despot." And, "Until an actor is at home in his dress he is not at home in his part!"

° The reigning authority for mass education in Victorian times

Quoting Hegel's system of contraries, he ends his "theatrical essay," "In Art there is no such thing as an Universal Truth. A Truth in Art is that whose contradictory is also true."

He concluded with "Not that I agree with everything that I have said in this essay—there is much with which I entirely disagree!"

To understand the theater—if not Wilde himself—one could do worse than read or reread "The Truth of Masks." As well as wisdom and acerbic truths, it is full of smiles.

Wilde's two sons, Cyril and Vyvyan, were six and four-and-a-half years old respectively when *Intentions* pitched the literary world of the time into something like disarray; simultaneously he was being attacked for his novel, *The Picture of Dorian Gray*. Virtually the entire British press condemned *Dorian Gray* and its author. The wan face of Victorian England, alarmed at Wilde's contempt of the established and conventional form of bland, "virtuous" fiction, scowled angrily behind a scabrous reality of vice, rampant venereal disease, child prostitution, cant, and hypocrisy. Newspapers shrieked: "Decadent!" "Immoral!" The *Daily Chronicle* spat, *"The Picture of Dorian Gray* is a tale spawned from the leprous literature of the French decadents," summing it up as "a poisonous book—heavy with the mephitic odours of moral and spiritual putrefaction. . . ."

Oscar Wilde smiled and rose vigorously to his own defense. He had always held that "A work of art must never be judged by any standards of morality, or by any ethical code with which it has nothing in common."

While the battle raged, the author fired salvo after cerebral salvo. But he had enraged the Establishment once again, and the Establishment would, in its own good time, "reap the Wilde wind"!

TIOBO-5

Oscar Wilde was a good and attentive father to his two sons. Visitors to Tite Street declared this his marriage to Constance appeared as "a soft, gentle, and comfortable relationship."

A regular visitor to the Wilde house was the effete Lord Alfred Bruce Douglas, third son of the eighth Marquis of Queensbury. The Marquis himself was notorious in London society as a despotic bully, a nobleman with a grudge against life who had an almost pathological hatred of his wife and children.

Lionel Pigot Johnston, a twenty-four-year-old friend, had introduced Lord Alfred to Wilde. Their friendship developed while on shared holidays abroad, at house parties, and at formal and informal functions and gatherings. Inevitably, Lord Alfred—nicknamed Bosie—was a regular companion at Oscar Wilde's table at the Café Royal and other epicurean venues. Oscar's friends soon accepted Bosie Douglas, even if some did not like him. From now on, there was to be the "beautiful boy" Bosie at Wilde's side.

Wilde was well aware that Lord Alfred was the only member of the Queensbury family to stand up to the obnoxious Marquis; indeed, Bosie had openly and publicly derided his father. It was not long before Bosie and Wilde learnt that "The Black Marquis"—as society had dubbed Queensbury—was conducting a vicious vendetta against Wilde in the social salons and gentlemen's clubs of London.

Wilde, however, chose to ignore the campaign of calumny and continued to bask in his own acclaim, with Lord Alfred rarely far from his side. He claimed that Bosie possessed literary attributes that appealed to him. Lord Alfred was a young and, many claimed, gifted poet of the sonnet form, and since his days at Trinity Wilde had long had a weakness for the sonnet.

Bosie's youth, beauty, and talent had a mesmeric effect on Wilde; additionally the boy belonged to one of Britain's oldest and most distinguished sporting families. (The rules pertaining to the correct procedures of boxing as a sport are to this day known in Britain as the Queensbury Rules).

Throughout Queensbury's campaign of vilification, Wilde conducted himself with considerable restraint and decorum. He was, however, angry when Queensbury forced himself on his presence at his Tite Street home, accompanied by a thick-set prize fighter! An angry scene ensued, with Queensbury accusing Wilde of conducting obscene practices with Lord Alfred. Wilde won the day; the Marquis left the house with the prizefighter escort, both lashed by Wilde's indignant verbal assault.

The unsolicited visit had been a calculated attempt at intimidation and Wilde was having none of it. Lord Alfred stood foursquare with Wilde against his father, and the two openly continued their friendship.

Little has been recorded of Constance's reaction to the Tite Street fracas. Queensbury continued his slander, but it is known that Constance remained steadfastly on the side of her husband; she continued to organize and conduct Oscar's Tite Street salon with her accustomed grace, elegance, and obvious affection for Oscar.

Wilde, for his part, remained as scintillating as ever, and received his illustrious guests not only at his home and at the Café Royal but often also in France and elsewhere on the Continent. He had met the threatened scandal decisively and had decided to ignore it thereafter. He spent much time with his artistic friends and, as might be expected, had some characteristic comments on them, their pursuits, foibles, fancies, and fantasies. Even modern "gods" were prone to have their legends punctured.

Here is a typical Wildean peroration of the time delivered on Wilde's meeting Richard Le Gallienne:

So you are going to see [Walter] Pater? That will be delightful. But I must tell you one thing about him to save you disappointment. You must not expect him to talk about his prose. Of course, no true artist ever does that. But Pater never talks about anything that interests him. He will not breathe one golden word about the Renaissance. No! He will probably say something like this: So you wear cork soles in your shoes? Is that really true? And do you find them comfortable? How extremely interesting!

There were, of course, those who hit back at Wilde. Earlier, probably because Oscar exuded the *Weltanschauung* of the intellectual who had been everywhere and met everybody worth meeting, he had been attacked by Ambrose Bierce, the eclectic author of *The Devil's Dictionary* and other works, as "That sovereign of insufferables." Even Yeats, an acknowledged admirer, was now critically abusive of the man and *his* mask: "His manner had hardened to meet opposition and at times he allowed one to see an unpardonable insolence. His charm was acquired and systematized, a mask which he wore only when it pleased him. . . ."

Years later Swinburne was to hit back cruelly with,

When Oscar came to join his God,
Not earth to earth, but sod to sod,
It was for sinners such as this
Hell was created bottomless.

Such Machiavellian malice had no part in Oscar's humor. Audacity, perhaps. But then who could resist "The three women I have most admired are Queen Victoria, Sarah Bernhardt, and Lily Langtry. I would have married any one of them with pleasure!"

His friend Robert Ross, in a letter to Adela Schuster, 23 December 1900, was perhaps closer to the truth than even Oscar would have been prepared to admit: "He was never quite sure himself where and when he was serious. . . ."

ON WRITERS AND WRITING

*Wit is as infinite as love, and a deal more
lasting in its qualities.*
—Agnes Repplier "A Plea For Humour"
Points of View, 1891

Like most celebrities, Wilde had enemies. How many is unknown, but it is known that most of his enemies emerged out of jealousy of his genius. Certainly, George Moore, the Irish novelist and author of *Esther Waters,* was one. Moore positively loathed his fellow Irishman and is on record as accusing Wilde of

> . . . paraphrasing and inverting the witticisms and epigrams of others. [His] method of literary piracy was on the lines of the robber Cacus, who dragged stolen cows backwards by the tails into his cavern so that their hooveprints might not lead to the detection of the robbery. . . .

This story was repeated to Wilde one evening at a private dinner party in Clarges Street. He was questioned by his host, a well-known politician, "Oscar, do you know this fellow Moore?" Wilde, ever ready with the apposite, astringent reply, repeated the question, "Do I know—him? Indeed, I know him so well that I have not spoken to him for ten years!" Shortly afterwards, when Moore's name came up again in conversation, Oscar pondered on it with a frown of vague familiarity. "Moore? George Moore?" he queried. "He was the fellow who wrote excellent English until he discovered grammar, wasn't he?" And Moore's book, *Esther Waters*, drew this Wildean comment: "He leads his readers to the latrine and locks them in."

Frank Harris once accused Wilde—but not to his face—of knowing nothing about painting, although Wilde had written a learned essay, "The English Renaissance of Art." Wilde may not have been an expert, but he knew what painters and painting he liked and was never averse to making comment on either as, when in conversation, he drew attention to "that curious mixture of bad painting and good intentions that always entitles a man to be called 'a representative British artist.' "

Characteristically, he enjoyed making fun of himself, such as the occasion when he was shown Frith's celebrated *Derby Day* oil canvas which was to be bought for the nation. Oscar looked hard at it and, with an air of disarming irreverence, enquired, "Is it really all done by hands?" And he later observed, with some accuracy, "No work of art ever puts forward views. Views belong to people who are not artists." "Artists, like gods, should never leave their pedestals," he wryly pontificated on another occasion.

Frank Harris, looking for Wilde at the Café Royal, was told that he had just left. He had apparently departed, leaving the message, "I was working on the proof of one of my poems all the morning, and took out a comma. This afternoon I put it back again!"; he was well aware of the truth that "A poet can survive anything but a misprint!"

There are those who claim that some of Wilde's poems were greatly influenced by the youthful Kipling. In "The East A'Callin'," Wilde's lines, lovely as they are, do echo an identifiable redolence of the style and technique of the author of "If":

> The almond groves of Samarkand,
> Bokhara, where red lilies blow,
> And Oxus, by whose yellow sand
> The grave white-turbanned merchants go;
>
> And on from thence to Ispahan,
> The golden garden of the sun,
> Whence the long dusty caravan
> Brings cedar and vermillion.

As was to be expected, poetry figured prominently in the Café Royal literary discussions, at one of which Wilde drawled, "When a man acts, he is a puppet. When he describes, he is a poet." The circle knew, too, of a certain Café Royal poet who claimed almost total versatility in his art; his poetry, he claimed, ranged from the immortality of the soul to the lilt of laughter. Wilde caustically observed, "We fear that he will never produce any really good work until he has made his mind whether destiny intends him for a poet or an advertising agent!"

When Wilde's volume of poetry, *In Memoriam*, was first published, it was a limited edition. Explaining this, Oscar disclosed, "My first idea was to print only three copies; one for myself, one for the British Museum, and one for Heaven. I had some doubt about the British Museum!" He was well aware that "One man's poetry is another man's poison," and such remarks linger, like his reply to another question, "Books of poetry by young writers are usually promissory notes that are never met."

Wilde, never diffident on the subject of his fellow poets, pronounced of Swinburne, "He is so eloquent that whatever he touches becomes unreal"; and on Dr. Robert Yelverton Tyrrell he was equally dismissive: "If he had known less, he would have been a poet." Neither was he highly complimentary of two other popular poets of his time. "Meredith," he declared, "is a prose Browning and so is Browning; he uses poetry as a medium for writing prose . . . ," and Whistler *had* to reemerge in further assessment, "Whistler, with all his faults, was never guilty of writing a line of poetry!"

It is important to underline that if many of Wilde's remarks, quips, observations, and verbal critiques appear to display an element often tantamount to insult, they were usually delivered with a whimsical smile. He well knew that such blistering wit was expected of him, and he confidently played to his audience.

On the subject of cheap, popular literature, which sold in vast quantities in Victorian times, Wilde placed his views firmly on record. "Shilling literature," he claimed, "is always making demands on our credulity without ever appearing to our imagination"; and he was quick to dismiss the romantic novel of that *oeuvre*. He summarized one with, "It could be read without any trouble and was probably written without any trouble also."

Wilde loathed the sanctimonious novelists of his day. "The aim of most of our modern novelists," he claimed, "seems to be not to write good novels, but rather to write novels that will do good"; but in "gentler" mood he took the view that "One should not be too severe on English novels; they are the only relaxation of the intellectually unemployed!"

Of his own work in the medium of the novel, he was crisp and frank. "I write," he said, "because it gives me the greatest possible artistic pleasure to do so. If my work pleases the few, I am gratified. If it does not, it causes me no pain. As for the mob, I have no desire to be a popular novelist. It is far too easy."

He discussed the craft of writing with Sir Arthur Conan Doyle, creator of Sherlock Holmes. Oscar explained his approach. "Between me and Life there is a mist of words always. I throw probability out of the window for the sake of a phrase, and the chance of an epigram makes me desert truth. . . . Still," he excused himself, "I do aim at making a work of art."

And those in the London literary set who were jadedly jealous of his success he dismissed with, "The basis of literary friendship is mixing the poisoned bowl."

Upon being shown an elaborate publication of Italian literature, he examined the volume closely, looked up, and observed, "This displays a want of knowledge that must be the result of years of study!"

Wilde was often gently upbraided for his hedonistic tastes. He explained these away with, "It is a duty we owe to the dignity of letters!" And few of his celebrated friends were above his amusingly abrasive appraisal. Remember that of the erstwhile Bernard Shaw, then an ascending "star," of whom Wilde had said, "Bernard Shaw is an excellent man. He has not an enemy in the world—and none of his friends like him!" Oscar once inquired of one of Max Beerbohm's closest friends, "Tell me, when you are alone with Max, does he take off his face and reveal his mask?"

A year before Wilde died, he displayed, in a letter to Robert Ross, further caustic disregard for the talents of America's Henry James, who—living in England—considered Americans a race superior to Europeans. "James is developing," Wilde wrote, "but he will never arrive at passion, I fear. . . ." And at a literary dinner, he accused Froude, "Like most penmen, you overrate the power of the sword."

His applause invariably came in the form of spontaneous laughter—and laughter he loved. Wilde's humor infected most of his audiences. Sometimes waspish, often dismissive, always penetrating, occasionally barbed, and invariably very funny, he had the God-given ability, as had the later Shaw, to make people laugh.

As was written of him during the Café Royal Centenary celebrations in 1965, "Wilde coined epigrams which were still repeated even when his serious work was in disfavor, such as at the time of the book publication of *The Picture of Dorian Gray*. Some were not the calculated result of verbal legerdemain, and one, at least, contained the essence of his own tragedy." That was the time when he declared with a hint of sadness, "The Cloister of the Café—there is my future. I tried the Hearth, but it was a failure. . . ."

He could be feliciously flattering, especially to those he admired, such as Aubrey Beardsley who had supplied decorations for the English translation of his *Salomé* in 1894. To this brilliant artist he once said, "When I have before me one of your drawings, I want to drink absinthe, which changes color like jade in sunlight and makes the senses thrall, and then I can live myself back in ancient Rome, in Rome of the later Caesars. . . ."

It has been recorded that Wilde only drank absinthe as "an aperitif and as a pose." Apart from hock and seltzer, his favorite drink was whiskey and soda—preferably Irish whiskey, doubtless partly out of patriotism and partly because, in the eighties and nineties, it was more popular than Scotch. But he had the ability to contain his liquor; he was rarely the worse for it.

Wilde was, of course, brilliantly adept at the put-down—the crushing, unanswerable reply. At a dinner party in the Café Royal given by the mendacious Frank Harris and attended by Max Beerbohm, Beardsley, Robert Ross, and Wilde, Harris monopolized the conversation with highly colored accounts of his social triumphs among London's aristocracy. Harris was probably the most uncrushable man of his day. It was Wilde who finally silenced him with the quietly delivered direct hit, "Yes, my dear Frank—you have dined in every house in London—once!"

Wilde had stated his belief that art had absolutely no effect on morality. It is worth repeating that he had gone further in Harris's *Saturday Review:* "Art is the only serious thing in the world. And the artist is the only person who is never serious." He was close to the truth when he averred, patently with tongue in cheek, "It is only an auctioneer who can equally and impartially admire all schools of art."

Wilde's friends and acolytes accepted his genius as a writer, but there were those in and around his circle who, no doubt clandestinely, sought to play down his legendary powers as a conversationalist, just as Harris decried his knowledge of art and music. But not William Butler Yeats, the distinguished Irish poet, leader of the Irish literary renaissance of his time, who well over thirty years later was to receive a Nobel Prize for literature.

Yeats first met Wilde at a party given by William Ernest Henley, the English poet and journalist who had collaborated with Robert Louis Stevenson. Yeats was to recall the meeting:

My first meeting with Oscar Wilde was an astonishment. I never before heard a man talking with perfect sentences, as if he had written them all overnight with labor and yet all spontaneous. . . .

There was present that night at Henley's, by right of propinquity or of accident, a man full of the secret spite of dullness, who interrupted from time to time, and always to check or disorder thought; and I noticed with what mastery he was foiled and thrown. I noticed, too, that the impression of artificiality that I think all Wilde's listeners have recorded came from the perfect rounding of the sentences and from the deliberation that made it possible. That very impression helped him, as the effect of meter, or of the antithetical prose of the seventeenth century, which is itself a true meter, helped its writers, for he could pass without incongruity, from some unforeseen, swift stroke of wit to elaborate reverie. I heard him say a few nights later, "Give me *The Winter's Tale,* Daffodils that come before the swallow dares, but not *King Lear.* What is *King Lear* but poor life staggering in the fog?" And the slow, carefully-modulated cadence sounded natural to my ears.

The first night he praised Walter Pater's *Studies in The History of The Renaissance*—"It is my golden book: I never travel anywhere without it; but it is the very flower of decadence; the last trump should have sounded the moment it was written. . . ."

That Oscar Wilde had the true power of real, spontaneous wit is shown by his happy retort to Sir Lewis Morris. Morris was complaining about the studied neglect of his personal claims when possible successors to the Poet Laureateship were being discussed after Tennyson's death in 1892. Said the disenchanted author of *The Epic of Hades,* "It is a complete conspiracy of silence against me—a conspiracy of silence! What ought I to do, Oscar?" Wilde's swift and smiling retort? "Join it!"

DORIAN GRAY
'LEPROUS LITERATURE'

Since when was Genius found respectable?
—Elizabeth Barrett Browning (1806-1861)

Wilde's book *The Picture of Dorian Gray* was published in 1891. In the face of vitriolic press attacks, the author brilliantly defended the work, rising above his critics. He applauded the judgment of his friends who expressed admiration of the book. To Ralph Payne he wrote, "I am so glad that you like that strange coloured book of mine. It contains much of me in it. Basil Hallward is what I think I am; Lord Henry what the world thinks me; Dorian what I would like to be—in other ages perhaps . . . ," words that contained an element of truth, for he had always vigorously held that for the creative writer, art has no boundaries.

In the running battle with his critics, he pointedly claimed his novel to be "a work of art." He accused some of his adversaries of personal malice and attacked their "inferior minds."

He justified his strange, hedonistic book as a work of "abstract contemporaneous characters." "Good people," he argued with force, "belonging as they do to the normal, and so commonplace, type, are artistically uninteresting." He dismissed as "a vulgar phrase" the words of one critic who accused him of "creating characters as mere catchpenny revelations of the non-existent." "Quite so," agreed the author. "If they existed, they would not be worth writing about. The function of the artist is to invent, not to chronicle. There are no such people. If there were, I would not write about them."

He claimed that *Dorian Gray* was "a story with a moral," the moral being, "All excess, as well as all renunciation, brings its own punishment, a moral which the prurient will not be able to find in it, but which will be revealed to all whose minds are healthy. Is this an artistic error?" He provided his own answer. "I fear it is. It is the only error in the book."

It was Wilde in full pursuit of Victorian hypocrisy and cant, the affected puritanism of a largely debauched society. Wilde was later brilliantly to defend the book again in a verbal battle with his one-time Trinity colleague, Edward Carson.

Whatever his critics thought of *Dorian Gray*, there is no doubt that Wilde's audacious wit achieved what he had claimed really amused him: "To entertain the working classes, to enrage the middle classes and to fascinate the aristocracy." He was certainly the first to admit in the novel that "The advantage of the emotions is that they lead us astray." Neither did he endear himself to the Establishment with, "The only difference between a caprice and a life-long passion is that the caprice lasts a little longer," clandestine caprices in highly respectable households being as common as in Victorian rat-infested hovels.

What was termed "romance," that lyrical-sounding state of the imagination, came in for its share of Wildean castigation: "When one is in love, one always begins by deceiving oneself, and one always ends up by deceiving others. That is what the world calls Romance." Characteristically, his wisdom was often the warrior of his wit. "Those who are faithful know only the trivial side of love; it is the faithless who know love's tragedies."

His overall view could be said to be summarized with this trenchant *Dorian Gray* dialogue: "In this country it is enough for a man to have distinction and brains for every common tongue to wag against him. And what sort of lives do these people who pose as being moral lead themselves? We are in the native land of the hypocrite"—a fluent echo of Lord Macaulay on the subject of the English race which Wilde, himself, dismissed as representing an age of "the survival of the pushing"; he also shot the critical rapids with this aside: "I don't desire to change anything in England except the weather." The rapier had penetrated the flesh of his critics and Wilde was ready to twist it in the wound. "There is no literary public in England for anything except newspapers, primers, and encyclopedias. Of all the people in the world, the English have the least sense of the beauty of literature."

Oscar Wilde was unrepentant, wallowing in his gleeful ability to stoke up controversy, which, he well knew, would result in the name and views of Oscar Wilde being still further discussed, castigated, or applauded.

He was a brilliant self-publicist. Who else of his era would have dared provocatively to pontificate, "There are only two kinds of people who are really fascinating—people who know absolutely everything and people who know absolutely nothing"? It was later to be said of him that he was more than familiar with both types. . . .

Yet, strangely, with his declared antipathy to shallowness, he included in his book the enigmatic line, "It is only the shallow people who do not judge by appearances." Perhaps he was right? He also considered, "One can always be kind to people about whom one cares nothing," and, with mellifluous phrasing, he was soon acquainting his readers with his preferences, "I like persons better than principles and I like persons with no principles better than anything else in the world!"

He, better than most, knew the intellectual essence of truth, but he wasn't giving all away. "If a man treats life artistically, his brain is in his heart." And one could certainly laugh with his character who opined, "The only artists I have ever known who are personally delightful are bad artists. Good artists exist simply in what they make and consequently are perfectly uninteresting in what they are."

The enigma of Wilde, the man and the artist, could be said to have deepened with, "One should absorb the colour of life, but one should never remember its details. Details are always vulgar!" And, "Every effect that one produces gives one an enemy. To be popular, one must be a mediocrity." But these are simply lines of dialogue by characters in *The Picture of Dorian Gray* and must be accepted as such. In another chapter, he added, "All art is at once surface and symbol. Those who go beneath the surface do so at their peril. Those who read the symbol do so at their peril."

His further contention that "To reveal art and conceal the artist is art's aim," if true, appears to stop just short of the metaphysical. Others, in popular parlance, claimed art to be merely the creative evidence of the artist! Be that as it may, Wilde's novel, consciously or subconsciously, contained in its dialogue a built-in rebuff to its severest critics: "The books that the world calls immoral are books that show the world its shame," in the same way as "It is the spectator, and not life, that Art mirrors."

Wilde never missed an opportunity to allow a character, as in *Dorian Gray*, to battle with his own previously expressed views, such as this volte-face: "We can forgive a man for making a useful thing as long as he does not admire it. The only excuse for making a useless thing is that one admires it intensely. All art is quite useless!"

He loved his own contradictory dialogue: "The only reason, indeed, that excuses one for asking any questions is simple curiosity!"

Ever the purist in the matter of words, Wilde, in *Dorian Gray*, repeatedly echoed his own attitudes. He was always prepared to attack the vulgar and unseemly. "I hate vulgar realism in literature. The man who could call a spade should be compelled to use one. It is the only thing he is fit for!"

Is this, too, Wilde's dialogue echoing the personal philosophy of Wilde, the writer? "There is only one thing in the world worse than being talked about, and that is not being talked about," a view shared by Bernard Shaw, who later repeated the phrase as his own. In similar paradox, Wilde opined, "No civilised man ever regrets a pleasure, and no uncivilised man ever knows what a pleasure is." And he was quite certain that "Nothing can cure the soul but the senses, just as nothing can cure the senses but the soul."

Discussing music, he was careful to check that the composer Richard Wagner had died in Venice some eight years earlier, before saying, "I like Wagner's music better than anybody's. It is so loud that one can talk the whole time without people hearing what one says!"

He was ready to explain his reactions to music:

> After playing Chopin, I feel as if I had been weeping over sins that I had never committed, and mourning over tragedies that were not my own. Music always seems to me to produce that effect. It creates for one a past of which one has been ignorant and fills one with a sense of sorrows that have been hidden from one's tears.

But if he shied away from music for these reasons, he recognized its value in art, in "The English Renaissance of Art," published in 1882:

Music is the art in which form and matter are always one, the art whose subject cannot be separated from the method of its expression, the art which most completely realises the artistic ideal, and is the condition to which all the other arts are constantly aspiring.

His inner appreciation of music took poetic wing in his "In the Gold Room—A Harmony":

> Her ivory hands on the ivory keys
> Strayed in fitful fantasy,
> Like the silver gleam when the poplar trees
> Rustle their pale leaves listlessly
> Or the drifting foam of restless sea
> When the waves show their teeth in the
> flying breeze. . . .

Music unquestionably stirred his imagination.

I can fancy a man who had led a perfectly commonplace life, hearing by chance some curious piece of music, and suddenly discovering that his soul, without his being conscious of it, had passed through terrible experiences, and known fearful joys, or wild romantic loves, or great renunciations. . . .

And again, in "The Burden of Itys," in 1881:

. . . a quality which music sometimes has which is most nigh to tears and memory . . .

Even near the end, in *The Ballad of Reading Gaol*, he remembered.

> It is sweet to dance to violins
> When Love and Life are fair:
> To dance to flutes, to dance to lutes
> Is delicate and rare:
> But it is not sweet with nimble feet
> To dance upon the air!

But if the inner man loved music, in *The Picture of Dorian Gray* he wasn't letting on. "If one hears bad music," he wrote, "it is one's duty to drown it by one's conversation." And in *An Ideal Husband* he pontificated, "Musical people are so absurdly unreasonable. They always want to be perfectly dumb at the very moment when one is longing to be absolutely deaf." His cynicism had already been marked in *The Importance of Being Earnest*. "If one plays good music," he had said, "people don't listen, and if one plays bad music, people don't talk." As far as acting was concerned, he confided, "I love acting. It is so much more real than life!" and added, "It is not good for one's morals to see bad acting!"

There are those who hold that this truism in *Dorian Gray* was an echo of self-inflicted criticism of the author: "The mind of a thoroughly well-informed man is a dreadful thing. It is like a bric-à-brac shop, all monsters and dust, with everything priced above its proper value."

In *Dorian Gray,* Wilde's constancy to the young knew no bounds.

> The pulse of youth that beats in us at twenty becomes sluggish. Our limbs fail, our senses rot. We degenerate into hideous puppets, haunted by the memory of the passions of which we were too much afraid and the exquisite temptations that we had not the courage to yield to. Youth! Youth! There is absolutely nothing in the world but Youth!

He could be devastatingly direct on the subject of poets and poetry, especially if his dialogue tilted securely with character and scene.

> A great poet, a really great poet, is the most unpoetical of creatures. But inferior poets are absolutely fascinating. The worse their rhymes, the more picturesque they look. The mere fact of having published a book of second-rate sonnets makes a man quite irresistible. He lives the poetry he cannot write. The others write the poetry that they dare not realise.

Wilde, even at the height of his fame, never succumbed to entreaties to write his autobiography. Had he done so, one is tempted to wonder how he would have approached it, for on that topic he had this to say: "The critic is he who can translate into another manner of a new material his impression of beautiful things. The highest, as the lowest, form of criticism is a mode of autobiography"; and how true his assessment that "The fatality of good resolutions is that they are always too late!"

As a skillful and accomplished writer, he well knew most of the pitfalls of his profession. He had admitted, "We can have in life but one great experience at best, and the secret of life is to reproduce that experience as often as possible." It was a maxim worth repeating and remembering. Yet, in Chapter Four of *Dorian Gray*, he did verbal battle with Experience even if not The Great Experience: "Experience is of no ethical value. It is merely the name men give to their mistakes!"

But what if mere mortals do not recognize The Great Experience when it happens? Well, we can take another Wildean view:

I never approve, or disapprove, of anything new. It is an absurd attitude to take towards life. We are not sent into this world to air our moral prejudices. I never take any notice of what common people say, and I never interfere with what charming people do.

Again, in Chapter Two, one of his characters expatiates, "He knew the precise psychological moment when to say nothing!"—an asset of unquestioned value.

If he had ever approved of the rural scene, he dismisses it contemptuously in *Dorian Gray*. "It is the pure unadulterated country life. They get up early because they have so much to do and go to bed early because they have so little to think about." But benevolence for Wilde the playwright overwhelms one's own carp when one of his actors delivers the line, "Whenever a man does a thoroughly stupid thing, it is always from the noblest motives!"

And what of the elusive secret of youth? He claimed to have found the answer: "To get back one's youth, one has merely to repeat one's follies!" So, in fashionable idiom, we're back to square one!

Wilde wrote brilliantly about men, but, as we know, he also penned a lot of droll throughts about women, categorizing them as voyeurs all: "A woman will flirt with anybody in the world as long as other people are looking on!" And those interested may be comforted to learn that "As long as a woman can look ten years younger than her own daughter, she is perfectly satisfied!" Wilde knew, too, the powers of the species. "Women," he said, "as some witty Frenchman once put it, inspire us with the desire to do masterpieces, and always prevent us from carrying them out!"

He fully recognized the many dangers and delights in the machinations of those on the distaff side. "I am afraid," he warned, "that women appreciate cruelty, downright cruelty, more than anything else. They have wonderfully primitive instincts. We have emancipated them, but they remain slaves looking for their masters all the same."

On friendship, he expounded, "Laughter is not at all a bad beginning for a friendship, and it is the far best ending for one!" It is a choice thought, too, that "One has the right to judge a man by the effect he has over his friends." He extended this pungently with, "I always like to know everything about my new friends, and nothing about my old ones!"

As far as relatives were concerned, his wit on this topic diverts the reading of *Dorian Gray*. "I can't help detesting my relations," Wilde wrote. "I suppose it comes from the fact that none of us can stand other people having the same faults as ourselves!" Wisdom from the bosom, so to speak!

On the subject of money, Wilde again came into his own.

"Credit," he claimed, "is the capital of a younger son." As for those *without* money, "I should fancy that the real tragedy of the poor is that they can afford nothing but self-denial!"

He could be indignantly apprehensive of human habits, as in this: "There are many things we would throw away if we were not afraid that others might pick them up"; but he was realist enough to hold that "When we are happy we are always good, but when we are good we are not always happy!"

Sin, murder, and scandal are recurring themes in Wilde's writings. For example, in *Dorian Gray,* he considers that "Murder is always a mistake . . . one should never do anything that one cannot talk about after dinner!" He accurately opined that "Sin is a thing that writes itself across a man's face. It cannot be concealed," a truism well evident in *Dorian Gray.* He was loath to leave the subject alone. "Nothing makes one so vain as being told that one is a sinner," he quipped. And one of his characters, with waspish equanamity, claimed of another, "You will soon be going about like the converted and the revivalist, warning people against all the sins of which you have grown tired!"

Wilde could be delightfully frivolous on the subject of scandal—especially scandal concerning others: "I love scandals about other people, but scandals about myself don't interest me. They have not got the charm of novelty"; and he was not prepared to permit scandal to rest in peace. "The basis of every scandal is an immoral certainty," he chirped, and further warned, "One should never make one's debut with a scandal. One should reserve that to give an interest to one's old age!"

He was risibly intolerant of the moral standards of his day: "Modern morality consists in accepting the standard's of one's age. I consider that for any man of culture to accept the standard of his age is a form of the grossest immorality."

As we have learned, he was no believer in Good Resolutions; was he too familiar with their fragility?

Good resolutions are useless attempts to interfere with scientific laws. Their origin is pure vanity. Their result is absolutely nil. They give us, now and then, some of those luxurious sterile emotions that have a certain charm for the weak. That is all that can be said of them.

That in one fell swoop cogently disposes of Good Resolutions!

What of belief? Oscar held the view that "As for believing things, I can believe anything provided that it is quite incredible!"

The tired, disenchanted cry of the much-pursued Adonis enters the dialogue via a morally dismembered Dorian: "I am sick of women who love me. Women who hate me are much more interesting." Disillusion often colored Wilde's philosophy. "The one charm of marriage," he averred, "is that it makes life a deception absolutely necessary for both parties." And he could not resist a sly dig at American marriages in particular: "Marriage is hardly a thing one can do now and then—except in America." Ennui, disenchantment—or both? "Love," he declared in the play, with total finality, "is an illusion."

Wilde, through his principal character, was pointedly partisan in his declaration that "The husbands of very beautiful women belong to the criminal classes." Was he suggesting that it is a crime to marry a beautiful woman?

He was ever disparaging, too, of actors as a class, although they often amused him. Most of those who worked with him in the theatre knew of his attitude. "As a rule," he declared, "people who act lead the most commonplace lives. They are good husbands or faithful wives, or something tedious. . . ."

Using medieval art as a dialogue device, he had this to say:

"Medieval art is charming, but medieval emotions are out-of-date. One can use them in fiction, of course. But then the only thing one can use in fiction are the things that one has ceased to use in fact!" But he underlined defiantly, "Youth is the one thing worth having."

Years later, Dr. Oliver St. John Gogarty,° Irish surgeon, writer, and wit, echoed and expounded on Wilde:

> This longing for youth, this dislike of old age is pre-eminently an Irish trait. Blind Raffery, the poet, who was born in Mayo but spent his days in Galway town, his face to the wall [i.e. blind], playing his music "to empty pockets" says, in the last line of his famous poem, "The County of Mayo," "Old age would never find me and I'd be young again." And in the twentieth century, Yeats in his "Seven Woods" tells how the squirrels rejoiced "As if they had been hidden in green boughs where old age cannot find them. . . ." The ancient Irish had no Valhalla in the heavens. They had their Land of Youth in their own country.

This was Wilde's obsession.

° *It Isn't This Time of the Year at All! An Unpremeditated Autobiography by Oliver St. John Gogarty.* MacGibbon & Kee, 1954.

AN IDEAL HUSBAND
—THE WIT AND THE LEGEND

*True wit is Nature to advantage dressed, What
oft was thought, but ne'er so well expressed.*
—ALEXANDER POPE *An Essay on Criticism*, 1711

Oscar Wilde's third comedy, *An Ideal Husband*, described by the management, Lewis Waller and H. H. Morell, as "A New and Original Play of Modern Life," was honored at its opening on 3 January 1895 by the Prince of Wales in the royal box with a complement of the British Court.

The Prince, who afterwards insisted that Wilde not change or delete a single word, let it be widely known that he thought the play "a sheer delight." The theatergoing public quickly formed their opinion, too. Heavy advance bookings indicated that Wilde had a major success on his hands.

Bernard Shaw applauded the piece with grace and generosity in the *Saturday Review:* "In a certain sense Mr. Wilde is to me our only thorough playwright. He plays with everything: with wit, with philosophy, with drama, with actors and audience, with the whole theatre." For his part, and with another stunning success to his credit, Wilde assumed his familiar air of studied indifference towards the rest of the critics.

An Ideal Husband boasted a fine cast: Alfred Bishop, Charles Hawtrey, Lewis Waller, Julia Neilson, Fanny Brough, Florence West, among other leading theatrical personalities. As might be expected, keen wit was the lance with which Wilde attacked society and its conventions, and again he bestrode his old hobby-horse of total rejection of vulgarity, not forgetting a dig or two at the English. "Vulgarity is simply the conduct of other people," he chortled. "The English can't stand a man who is always saying he is right, but they are very fond of a man who admits he has been in the wrong."

In character, he was bitchily witty when dealing with politicians. "In England," he jabbed, "a man who can't talk morality twice a week to a large, popular, immoral audience is quite over as a serious politician. There would be nothing left for him as a profession except Botany or the Church!" And he astringently preached, "To be pretty is the best fashion there is, and the only fashion that England succeeds in setting."

With total disdain of restraint, he swept on to echo his mother's views: "I love London Society! I think it has immensely improved. It is entirely composed now of beautiful idiots and brilliant lunatics. Just what Society should be!" Yet, in the same play, he had Lord Caversham, the archetypal aristocrat, grunting in huntin' English, "Can't make out how you stand London Society! The thing has gone to the dogs, a lot of damned nobodies talking about nothing!"

The play displayed Wilde at his best; it was a perfectly honed verbal point-counterpoint. His dialogue was of similar caliber when discussing even the less fortunate: "The . . . extraordinary thing about the lower classes in England—they are always losing their relations. They are extremely fortunate in that respect!" Relations seemed to be his *bête noire,* as often was society itself.

And he wouldn't let the English leave quietly, either. He had Mrs. Cheveley crow, "A typical Englishman—always dull and usually violent!" He cuttingly referred to "The English young lady—she is the dragon of good taste."

It might have been Wilde talking of life at Tite Street when one of his characters claimed, "I'm sure I don't know half the people who come to my house. Indeed, from all I hear, I shouldn't like to!"

There were, and doubtless still are, many who applauded his epigram, "Only dull people are brilliant at breakfast," and he was the first and, theatrically, not the last to assail his audience with, "To be natural is such a very difficult pose to keep up!"

How did the man do it? You may well ask. "Questions are never indiscreet. Answers sometimes are!" he declared, and similarly, with cryptic hauteur, "It is always worth while asking a question, though it is not always worth while answering one!"

Here he is again, peerlessly epigrammatic as ever:

Philanthrophy seems to me to have become simply the refuge of people who wish to annoy their fellow creatures.

If there was less sympathy in the world there would be less trouble in the world!

A sally of simple but apposite wisdom.

On the Victorian habit of formal calls on friends and acquaintances, he pronounced, "When one pays a visit, it is for the purpose of wasting other people's time, not one's own," then rudely admitted, "The most comfortable chair is the one I use myself when I have visitors," and clinching the visiting theme, "It is always nice to be expected and not to arrive."

On his philosophy of life and pastimes, he dealt this hand: "One should always play fairly—when one has the winning cards!"

An Ideal Husband was an ideal vehicle for this jaunty quip: "I don't like principles—I prefer prejudices!"; and he admitted, "I always pass on good advice. It is the only thing to do with it. It is never any use to oneself!"

With innate aloofness, Lady Basildon in the play disdainfully declares, "Ah! I hate being educated!" with which Mrs. Marchmont enthusiastically agrees, "So do I. It puts one almost on a level with the commercial classes!"

Wilde at his most philosophic could leave most university dons at the starting post—"Nothing ages like happiness"—just as he could be devastatingly deprecating to the rest of the community: "Other people are quite dreadful. The only possible society is one's self!"

Pinpointing no god in particular, the author of *An Ideal Husband*, in Act Two, wasn't exactly sympathetic to the pastimes of the devout: "When the gods wish to punish us they answer our prayers!"

Characteristically, plenty of wisdom dented the frothy dialogue of the play. "No man is rich enough to buy back his past," he quipped, and, with typical Wildean panache, completely bowled the fair sex with, "She wore far too much rouge last night and not quite enough clothes. That is always a sign of despair in a woman!" He repeated the dose with, "One should never give a woman anything she can't wear in the evening!"

Women were his verbal playthings. If there be doubt, try this: "She looks like a woman with a past. Most pretty women do!" But he did occasionally take up the cudgels on behalf of the ladies. "Women," he declared, "are never disarmed by compliments. Men always are. That is the difference between the sexes!" And as if further definition was required, he continued, "A woman's life revolves in curves of emotion. It is upon lines of intellect that a man's life progresses."

As ever, his total adoration of youth remained in the fore. "Youth isn't an affectation," he philosophized. "Youth is an art." And his social advice rarely went amiss. "An acquaintance that begins with a compliment is sure to develop into a real friendship. It starts in the right manner!"

He could summarize character in the upper echelons with uncanny accuracy: "He rides in the Row at ten o'clock in the morning, goes to the Opera three times a week, changes his clothes at least five times a day, and dines out every night of the Season. You don't call that leading an idle life, do you?" And his studied perception of others was faultless in its drollery: "He has one of those terribly weak natures that are not susceptible to influence." With even greater perception, he inquired, "How many men are there in modern life who would like to see their past burning to white ashes before them?"

There's laughter, too, in his line in *An Ideal Husband* that alleged, "There are terrible temptations that it required strength, strength and courage, to yield to. . . ."

How he loved to return again and again to women, albeit this time with a sally that quickly found a chink in the feminine armor: "Women are not meant to judge us, but to forgive us when we need forgiveness. Pardon, not punishment, is their mission"; and this thematic favorite is in barbed evidence again in the play: "In the case of very fascinating women, sex is a challenge, not a defense!"

Wilde, on hearing a Whistler aphorism, had earlier admitted, "I wish I'd said that!" to which Whistler had replied, "You will, Oscar, you will!" There are many who would like to have written, "There's only one real tragedy in a woman's life. The fact that her past is always her lover, and her future invariably her husband!" or, "Women are either hunting for husbands or hiding from them!"

Wilde's "theatrical honesty" shone through scene after scene of *An Ideal Husband*. "If we men married the women we deserve, we should have a very bad time of it!" But wouldn't the reverse be equally true?

That touch of music hall comedy mentioned earlier is evident as well in the play—"There is nothing so difficult to marry as a large nose!"—but we can speedily swing back to the sophisticated Wilde: "Once a week is quite enough to propose to anyone, and it should always be done in a manner that attracts some attention!"

Was Wilde talking of himself in self-deprecating mood, when in the play he opines, "I am not at all romantic. I am not old enough. I leave romance to my seniors"? But he soon returned with this mordant jest, "Morality is simply the attitude we adopt towards people whom we personally dislike!"

He penned the beautifully constructed maxim, "It is not the perfect but the imperfect who have need of love."

We leave *An Ideal Husband* with a delicious exchange between Mrs. Cheveley and Lady Markby:

Mrs. Cheveley: . . . their husbands! That is the one thing the modern woman never understands.
Lady Markby: And a very good thing, too, dear, I dare say. It might break up many a happy home if they did!

Brave, brave words—well and truly spoken.

"A TRIVIAL COMEDY
FOR SERIOUS PEOPLE"

Wit is the epitaph of an emotion.
—Friedrich Nietzsche
Miscellaneous Maxims and Opinions, 1897

The last—and perhaps the best—play written by Oscar Wilde was *The Importance of Being Earnest,* penned in a rented house on the esplanade at Worthing, on the south coast of England, where he was accompanied by Constance and their sons. He wrote it in three weeks during the month of September as a four-act play. He called it *Lady Lancing.* By the time he got around to sending it to actor-manager George Alexander, he had decided to retitle it *The Importance of Being Earnest.*

Wilde described the play as a farcical comedy. He cunningly sent it to Alexander, saying it was plainly unsuitable for him and would be of no interest, knowing full well that Alexander would take the flippant bait and jump at the chance not only to present it but to play the role of the polished John Worthing. Alexander, as Wilde knew, was his own favorite matinee idol!

He was unhappy with Alexander's expressed view that *The Importance of Being Earnest* should be cut from four to three acts. Alexander was forever watching the pennies, although his excuse was his desire to include a short one-acter, so popular as a "curtain-raiser" in those days. Alexander's carefulness may have sprung from his having started life as a clerk in a draper's warehouse. In any event, Wilde was reluctantly forced to agree, but took the trouble to let Alexander know of the "supreme sacrifice" he was making:

> Do you realise, Alec, what you are asking me to sacrifice? The act you are convinced is superfluous cost me terrible exhausting labour, not to mention heart-rending, nerve-racking strain. You may not believe me, but I assure you on my honour that it must have taken me fully five minutes to write it!

The three-act comedy opened at the St. James's Theatre, London, on 14 February 1895, boasting a distinguished cast headed by Alexander in the male lead, with seasoned stalwarts like Allan Aynesworth, Frank Dyall, Irene Vanbrugh, and H. H. Vincent.

Wilde had subtitled the play "A Trivial Comedy for Serious People"; some would have called it a blisteringly funny attack on the manners and morals of the aristocracy of the time. Wilde himself, when asked to describe his new play, replied, "The first act is ingenious, the second beautiful, the third abominably clever!" False modesty never inhibited *his* judgment of his own skills!

"Good looks," he truthfully opined in the play, "are a snare that every sensible man would like to be caught in," and amusingly had Miss Prism declare, "A misanthrope I can understand—a womanthrope, never!"

Here, again, was the beautifully disciplined wit on the rampage. "Thirty-five is a very attractive age; London society is full of women of the highest birth who have, of their own free choice, remained thirty-five for years!" he declared. With caustic, if not callous, diffidence he threw away, "To lose one parent, may be regarded as a misfortune; to lose both looks like carelessness!" And on parents in general, he held that "few pay any regard to what their children say to them. The old-fashioned respect for the young is fast dying!" It sounded as if he hadn't much regard for relatives, either: "Relations are simply a tedious pack of people who haven't the remotest knowledge of how to live, nor the smallest instinct about when to die!"

With unerring instinct he returned to the subject of women. "All women become like their mothers. That is their tragedy. No man does. That's his!"

He bemoaned the problems of the wealthy Victorian landowners. "Between the duties expected of one during one's lifetime, and the duties extracted from one after one's death, land has ceased to be either a profit or a pleasure!" But he did concede, "It is very vulgar to talk about one's business. Only people like stockbrokers do that, and then merely at dinner parties."

Taste invariably counseled his every line of dialogue, even when, as was so often the case, he chose to twist its tail: "Good taste is the excuse I've always given for leading such a bad life!" And his dialogue slid easily from laugh to laugh: "I hope you have not been leading a double life, pretending to be wicked and being really good all the time. That would be hypocrisy!" With mock morality he took the view that "It is a terrible thing for a man to find out suddenly that all his life he has been speaking nothing but the truth!"

The Importance of Being Earnest displayed Wilde's dialogue, wit, and theatrical construction at their brilliant best. With clipped emphasis, one of his characters declared, "The only way to behave to a woman is to make love to her if she is pretty, and to someone else if she is plain!" Another character rolled his tongue around this palpable hit: "The very essence of romance is uncertainty. If ever I get married, I'll certainly try to forget the fact!"

Wilde insisted on correct standards of behavior; but not without gaiety does Lady Bracknell put John Worthing through the mincer when he wants to marry her daughter:

> I would strongly advise you, Mr. Worthing, to try to acquire some relations as soon as possible and to make a definite effort to produce at any rate one parent, of either sex, before the Season is quite over. . . .

Wilde often referred in his plays to diaries, handling the "intimate" subject matter with dialogue that brought forth gales of laughter. For instance, "I never travel without my diary. One should always have something sensational to read in the train!" And on traveling itself—however short the distance—"You can't go anywhere without meeting clever people. The thing has become an absolute public nuisance. I wish to goodness we had a few fools left!"

In February 1895, Wilde was discussing *The Importance of Being Earnest* with Arthur Humphreys. He described it with his usual risible brilliance: "It is a play—written by a butterfly for butterflies"; but, as he well knew and said in the play, "The truth is rarely pure and never simple. Modern life would be very tedious if it were either, and modern literature a complete impossibility."

There was frequently the lucid wisdom of Wilde the poet in his lines: "What seems to us bitter trials are often blessings in disguise." But wit, above all, was the cutting edge, as when, in *The Importance of Being Earnest,* Cecily says, "When I see a spade, I call it a spade," and Gwendolene replies, "I am glad to say I have never seen a spade. It is obvious that our social spheres have been widely different!"

Wit always, and frequently sinewy wisdom. "My duty as a gentleman has never interfered with my pleasures in the smallest degree." If that be not your kind of wisdom, you might settle for this, in slightly lower key: "Memory is the diary that we all carry about with us," or, as a final sally in Act Two, "The good ended happily, the bad unhappily. That is what fiction means!" Alas, the future determined that Oscar Wilde was to be compelled, in salutary circumstances, *sans* fiction, to enlarge on that encapsulating definition.

His prolific output of plays, fairy tales, short stories, poems in prose, essays, short and long poems (e.g., *The Ballad of Reading Goal),* not to mention published letters and criticisms, constitute a formidable track record of literary versatility into most of which—with the exception of his poems—the deadly apposite epigram, the parabolic paradox, among many literary devices, are happily and frequently evident. In "The Portrait of Mr. W. H.," for example, "A thing is not necessarily true because a man dies for it," and, "It is always an advantage not to have received a sound commercial education." In contrast are thoughts (autobiographical?) culled from "The Remarkable Rocket," one of his enchanting fairy tales: "I like hearing myself talk. It is one of my greatest pleasures. I often have long conversations all by myself, and I am so clever that sometimes I don't understand a single word of what I am saying!"

With the same inventiveness, there reemerges that old echo of disenchantment, accompanied as always by wit: "Any place you love is the world to you—but love is not fashionable any more; the poets have killed it. They wrote so much about it, that nobody believed them, and I am not surprised!"

And how about this for cynicism enshrined in the guise of a fairy tale: "I dare say that if I knew him I should not be his friend at all. It is a very dangerous thing to know one's friends." And, again, "A sensitive person is one who, because he has corns himself, always treads on other people's toes!" Could this, too, be a Wildean autobiographical rumination? "I am always thinking about myself, and I expect everybody else to do the same. That is what is called sympathy."

Wilde, enclosed in his theatrical Never-Never land, was ever incorrigible, and delightfully so. "I like to do all the talking myself," he mused. "It saves time and prevents arguments!" and in another of his stories, "The Model Millionaire," "Romance is the privilege of the rich, not the profession of the poor," counterpointed by, "It is better to have a permanent income than to be fascinating." Few would disagree; the almighty dollar and the penurious pound still retain their own fascinations.

Back to another Wildean "fairy story," this time "The Devoted Friend," which echoes a philosophy lived out by the author himself: "I think that generosity is the essence of friendship," and in the same fairy tale he uttered a truism often ignored for reasons of convenience, "What is the good of friendship if one cannot say exactly what one means?"

In yet another singularly delightful fairy tale, "The Nightingale and The Rose," his acerbity is again aimed at actresses: "She is like most artists; she is all style without any sincerity."

Since we have not space to include all the wit and humor in Wilde's published writings, we cannot do worse than briefly return to "Lord Arthur Savile's Crime," a "comedy of murder" if you please, produced aeons before the descriptive theatrical device became a popular and overused motivation of stage humor. In this, the author deftly planted a familiar clue. "An inordinate passion for pleasure is the secret of remaining young," and those bristly relatives turn up again in "No one cares about distant relations nowadays. They went out of fashion years ago!" As for the popular cult of Puritanism, here is "Puritanism is not a theory of life. It is an explanation of the English middle-classes, that is all."

An excuse by Wilde is never less than delightful: "If a woman can't make her mistakes charming, she is only a female . . . ," and then the barb, "To be perfectly proportioned is a rare thing in an age when so many women are either over life-size or insignificant!"

Had he been flesh-and-blood, Lord Arthur himself would have found this audacious line to be vintage Oscar Wilde: "The proper basis for marriage is a mutual misunderstanding!" and, in a similar context, "Surely Providence can resist temptation by this time!" has all the essence of near-perfect satire, as has "Nothing looks so like innocence as an indiscretion!"

Wilde was not beyond paraphrasing Shakespeare, with bold effect. "The world," he noted, "is a stage, but the play is badly cast!"

Occasionally, the serious literary critic, in an analytical mood, becomes unconsciously as amusing as the writer he subjects to criticism. Hear, for example, Professor Richard Ellmann in his book, "The Artist as Critic," on Wilde and the wonder of his words:

. . . yet this ethical or almost ethical view of art coexists in Wilde with its own cancellation. He could write *Salomé* with one hand, dwelling on incest, and necrophilia, and show them as self-defeated, punished by execution and remorse. With the other hand he could dissolve by the critical intellect all notions of sin and guilt. He does so in *The Importance of Being Earnest,* which is all insouciance where *Salomé* is all incrimination. . . . In *The Importance of Being Earnest,* sins which are presented as accursed in *Salomé* and unnameable in *Dorian Gray,* are translated into a different key, and appear as Algernon's inordinate and selfish craving for—cucumber sandwiches(!) The substitution of mild gluttony for fearsome lechery renders all vice harmless.

Well, there's something to think about—especially the symbolism of the cucumber sandwiches!

WILDE AND SOCIALISM

*The renown of great men should always be
measured by the means which they have used
to acquire it.*

—Duc de La Rochefoucauld *Maxims,* 1665

Wilde, with his elitist intellect, esoteric mode of living, and life of salon and soirée, could hardly be expected to display much sympathy or overt understanding of the underdog of his day. He was an unashamed snob and an epigrammist of achievement superior to that of even the brilliant La Rochefoucald of the seventeenth century. Ugliness in any form was repellent to him, and this must have included the squalor of huge areas of Victorian destitution involving large families and appalling surroundings. It was not Wilde's customary playground.

Shaw, of course, with his early flight to the Fabians, the socialist intellectual society, was well aware of the gross inequality of the society of his youth and early manhood. It is to Shaw's credit that throughout most of his years he and some of his vocal fellow countrymen campaigned fearlessly in one form or another for better living and working conditions for the poor and socially deprived. With characteristic courage, Shaw lectured and wrote vigorously on socialism, on the desirability of an equal society.

Wilde was not that kind of animal. He sprang from upper-class, if somewhat penurious, stock. He was persuaded to attend a Fabian lecture given by Shaw. There is little doubt that Shaw, and the expressed vision of his socialist Utopia, made a surprising impression on Wilde, an impression subscribed to by his friend Robert Ross. What else could have induced Wilde, the heady hedonist, to pen his remarkable essay, "The Soul of Man Under Socialism?"

It should be emphasized that Wilde was careful not to advocate directly in this brilliantly witty examination of Shaw's and others' doctrinal diatribes any sort of revolutionary metamorphosis for the Britain of the late eighteen-hundreds. But his studied, intellectual arguments, indicating the desirability for a better deal for the poor and underprivileged throughout the country, did have a seam of sincerity. Certainly, when it was published, it did not endear him to his affluent, upper-class friends within the influential salon society of his day. His potent but never pleading arguments for "social reform" were underlined with characteristic wit. "The evolution of man is slow. The injustice of man is great," he wrote, but socialism as evinced in the Russia of the day, which he had derided in his first play, *Vera, or The Nihilists*, was a *non sequitur* for any sort of immediate application in Britain: "A Russian who lives happily under the present system of government in Russia must either believe that man has no soul or that, if he has, it is not worth developing." Not exactly a Fabian view!

Wilde's pungent humor shone through with considerable force in "Agitators are a set of interfering, meddling people, who come down to some perfectly contented class of the community and sow the seeds of discontent amongst them. That is the reason why agitators are so absolutely necessary!"

"The Soul of Man Under Socialism" was highly individualistic, a tract of power and positivism, a pointing precursor of things to come. Even the Tsarist Soviets read it, albeit with indigestion. It achieved a clandestine circulation in Russia that brought discomfort to the old and inspiration to the young. For who, even among those in coldest Siberia, could resist the barb, "All authority is quite degrading. It degrades those who exercise it, and it degrades those over whom it is exercised!" or, "It is to be regretted that a portion of our community should be practically in slavery, but to propose to solve the problem by enslaving the entire community is childish."

As a final, crushing denunciation of a life Wilde himself embraced in all its glittering affluence, was he really sincere in asserting, "If the Socialism is Authoritarian; if there are Governments armed with economic power as they are now with political power, if, in a word, we are to have Industrial Tyrannies, then the last state of man will be worse than the first"?

Inevitably, the position of the artist under the yoke of governmental power came in for penetrating disquisition: "People sometimes enquire what form of government it is most suitable for an artist to live under. To this question there is only one answer. The form of government that is most suitable to the artist is no government at all!" And he reflected that "The past is of no importance. The present is of no importance. It is the future that we have to deal with. For the past is what man should not have been. The present is what man ought not to be. The future is what artists are!"

As incisive as ever, Wilde knew precisely what he wanted to say and said it in his own gifted way, aware that scores of his readers would chucklingly recognize not only his wit but also his wisdom. Extensions of socialism could, in his view, prove monstrous, the begetter of totally unacceptable social atrocities. He put it simply: "To make men Socialists is nothing, but to make Socialism human is a great thing."

Throughout his essay, Wilde flayed those who were unjust in thought and activity, but he would not permit the artist to remain cornered, cowering in a pseudo-Utopian conception of a higher form of Marxism, the individual servile to the State: "A true artist takes no notice whatever of the public. The public to him are non-existent. He leaves that to the popular novelist!"

But did it all really matter? Wilde had his Theme and his Platform. And he knew that, however indigestible, whatever he thought and wrote would be avidly read. Socialism? The "threat" (as it was then described) was familiar enough, even in the esoteric area of poetry. "We have been able to have fine poetry in England because the public do not read it, and consequently do not influence it!" But was this entirely true?

According to Wilde it was, and art, he maintained, was infinitely more important than politics or any other "ism" of his time. "Art is the most intense mode of individualism that the world has known," he declared, awaiting the expected applause and disagreement.

One could accuse Wilde of many inconsistencies in his writings and verbal argument, but *never* inconsistency in his own defense of art and the artist, except when he was having fun with his theme. "When the public say a work is grossly unintelligible, they mean that the artist has said or made a beautiful thing that is new. When they describe a work as grossly immoral, they mean that the artist has said or made a beautiful thing that is true."

He held to long-expressed views, even in his "political" dissertations in "The Soul of Man Under Socialism:" "The public have an insatiable curiosity to know everything, except what is worth knowing." And with truth he held that "To live is the rarest thing in the world. Most people exist—that is all."

Man—in the guise of socialist, sinner or saint—was often a

contemptuous animal. In his view, "Vulgarity and stupidity are two very vivid facts in modern life. One regrets them, naturally. But there they are!"

He is on record as abhorring, and this in the late nineteenth century, what might nowadays be described as "intrusion" by means of the biographic device. "The private lives of men and women should not be told to the public. The public have nothing to do with them at all."

Alas, too few were to respect the axiom in relation to Oscar himself. After the turn of the century, the public was inundated by Wilde biographies, "revelations," pseudo-autobiographies and the like. In fairness, it must be said that for many years Wilde encouraged journalists to transpose the more glamorous and provocative aspects of his life into newspaper and magazine coverage for the edification and amusement of his avid public; he certainly did nothing to divert such interest. Be that as it may, with his customary charm and wit he was prepared to enlarge on his attitudes relating to man—this time espousing his views on crime and punishment: "A man cannot always be estimated by what he does. He may keep the law, and yet be worthless. He may break the law and yet be fine." Yes, here he was, back on his recurrent theme of crime and the criminal. "Starvation," he averred, "and not sin, is the parent of modern crime." Remembering the privation of large numbers of not-so-eminent Victorians, *that* probably touched a nerve!

Throughout his essay he had, as Professor Ellmann claims, "opposed suffering, yet acknowledged that the Russian novelists had rediscovered a great medieval theme, the (true) realisation of Man through suffering." This view seemed to obsess Wilde's intellectual approach to art and man's place in art during his time at University and his halcyon days as a successful writer, playwright, and poet.

In "The Soul of Man Under Socialism" he voiced the unequivocal view, "After all, even in prison a man can be quite free." He did not, however, countenance the view that the deprived were entirely blameless for their unhappy position in society. "There is only one class in the community that thinks more about money than the rich, and that is the poor. The poor can think of nothing else." He might have added, "Who can blame them?"

But trust Oscar to seek to justify his often outrageous comments with a paralyzing paradox, "As for begging, it is safer to beg than to take, but it is finer to take than to beg!"

It has to be conceded, though, that he *was* concerned with treasures other than gold: "Ordinary riches can be stolen from a man. Real riches cannot. In the treasure-house of your Soul, there are infinitely precious things that may not be taken from you." He enlarged on his theme with, "A red rose is not selfish because it wants to be a red rose. It would be horribly selfish if it wanted all the other flowers in the garden to be both red and roses." That is perhaps the simplest, most efficacious, and most unanswerable "political" argument to be published since the advent of that other less sibilant symbol of scarlet, the Red Flag.

Was it what today we call the plea of communism that Wilde summed up with the cryptic but all-revealing axiom that "Cultivated leisure is the aim of man"? Might we not do well to remember that, like most things in life, even leisure, cultivated or uncultivated, usually has to be worked and paid for. . . .

THE WIT OF WITS?

Wit makes its own welcome and levels all distinctions.

—Ralph Waldo Emerson
"The Comic," *Letters & Social Aims*, 1876

The *Oxford English Dictionary* boasts perhaps the clearest and most precise definition of wit: "that quality of speech or writing which consists in the apt association of thought and expression calculated to surprise and delight by its unexpectedness. . . ." Can one do better than that—especially in respect of Oscar Wilde's unique talent?

Many minds have applied themselves to definitions of the quicksilver quality of humor displayed in virtually everything Wilde said and wrote. His inventive talents never deserted him in a moment of need as, for example, in his essay "The Critic as Artist":

To be good, according to the vulgar standards of goodness, is obviously quite easy. It merely requires a certain amount of sordid terror, a certain lack of imaginative thought and a certain low passion for middle-class respectability. . . .

There had been those, including the erudite Voltaire who, in *Philosophical Dictionary*, published in 1764, had denigrated his contemporary purveyors of wit with, "He who cannot shine by thought, seeks to bring himself into notice by a witticism." But Voltaire's pronouncement could in no sense later apply to Wilde and his work; Wilde's intellect was infinitely superior to that of most of his contemporaries. Even Mark Twain's definition of wit quails in comparison to Wilde's polished polemics. As the American storyteller defined it, "Wit is the sudden marriage of ideas which before their union were not perceived to have any relation."

Shakespeare, for his part, certainly touched a truth in *Hamlet:* "Brevity is the soul of wit"; but he could not have anticipated that over two hundred and fifty years after he wrote these words, a wit of supreme ability would give the lie to his *dictat*; for Wilde could often be infinitely wordy, but he remained always extremely funny. He did not, as far as I can discover, define wit, but wit certainly defined him!

It may be difficult to accept Nietzsche's observation, in his *Miscellaneous Maxims and Opinions,* that "Wit is the epitaph of an emotion." It bears an element of truth, but does little to define the overall essence of true wit.

George Santayana in *The Sense of Beauty*, in 1896, certainly applied a touch of the sardonic to *his* definition, "The quality of wit inspires more admiration than confidence," which may well have been so; but as we leap to the 1920s we encounter André Maurois in his *De la Conversation,* touching an exposed nerve. "It is not enough to possess wit. One must have enough of it to avoid having too much. . . ." Oscar Wilde would have agreed, as he undoubtedly did with the thought contained in Alexander Pope's *An Essay of Criticism*, written in 1711: "True wit is Nature to advantage dress'd/What oft was thought, but ne'er so well expressed. . . ," while Sa'di, in 1258 (*Gulistan*) was disapproving of the social asset: "To be over much facetious is the accomplishment of courtiers and blemish of the wise." But perhaps his sense of humor was not over-much developed?

Again, Agnes Repplier, a contemporary of Wilde's, in her 1891 essay "A Plea For Humour" in *Points of View,* was at least descriptive in her definition: "Wit is as infinite as love, and a deal more lasting in its qualities." And perhaps Walter Savage Landor reached the periphery of accurate definition in his "Diogenes and Plato" (*Imaginary Conversations,* circa 1824): "What is perfectly true is imperfectly witty."

Landor hit the nail squarely on the head with, "True wit, to every man, is that which falls on another," while La Rouchefoucauld, in his *Maxims,* 1665, might well have been true of his time in holding, as he did, "The greatest fault of a penetrating wit is to go beyond the mark."

Certainly this was not true of Wilde. He always measured his intellectual distance. He could, as we have seen, use his mordant wit with telling effect, particularly against the male of the species, as in *Dorian Gray:* "Ernest Harrowden, one of those middle-aged mediocrities so common in London clubs, who have no enemies but are thoroughly disliked by their friends. . . ," adding, in *A Woman of No Importance,* "if he is a gentleman, he knows quite enough, and if he is not a gentleman, whatever he knows is bad for him. . . ." True wit, indeed, displaying an elasticity of intellect that converted an otherwise banal thought into a barbed aphorism, as again, "Women represent the triumph of matter over mind, just as men represent the triumph of mind over morals."

There was little appreciation of "do-gooders" in Wilde's makeup, if we are to believe him in Act I of *Lady Winder-*

mere's Fan: "I am afraid that good people do a great deal of harm in this world. Certainly the greatest harm they do is that they make badness of such extraordinary importance."

Oscar was an old hand at proffering advice on most worldly (and certain unworldly) subjects. "Talk to every woman as if you loved her," he counseled, "and to every man as if he bored you, and at the end of your first Season you will have the reputation of possessing the most perfect social tact!"

That his wit was masterly, if not incomparable, cannot be denied: it is perhaps epitomized in a remark he made to Laurence Housman when discussing religion, "Prayer must never be answered, if it is, it ceases to be prayer and becomes a correspondence!"

The mental agility of the true wit is a rare enough phenomenon in any age; I suspect that Wilde was much influenced in his acerbic talents by that "profligate parson," the inimitable Sydney Smith (1771-1845), Wilde's only rival in the area of real humor in the late eighteenth and early nineteenth centuries. Smith would have agreed when, of the Church, Wilde said, "The growth of common sense in the English Church is a thing very much to be regretted. It is really a degrading concession to a low form of reality." Indeed, had Smith been alive when Wilde wrote that in his essay "The Decay of Lying," the playwright would surely have been vigorously applauded by "The Smith of Smiths," for Sydney, although a cleric, abhorred the hypocrisy of many aspects of the the established Protestant church, as well as that of many *littérateurs*. Hadn't Smith proclaimed, "Macaulay has occasional flashes of silence that makes his conversation perfectly delightful"?

It was Smith, too, who provided literature not only with his justly celebrated *Letters of Peter Plymley* but also with what is perhaps a matchless analysis of wit and humor of clarity and sense. He wrote,

It is imagined that wit is a sort of inexplicable visitation, that it comes and goes with the rapidity of lightning, and that it is quite as unattainable as beauty or just proportion. . . . I am so much of a contrary way of thinking, that I am convinced a man might sit down as systematically and as successfully to the study of wit as he might to the study of mathematics: and I would answer for it that by giving up only six hours a day to being witty he should come on prodigiously before midsummer, so that his friends should hardly know him again. . . .

In short, you can *learn* to become a wit, provided you work at it hard enough. Presumably the same is true for the art of humor.

As you increase the incongruity, you increase the humor; as you diminish it, you diminish the humor.
If a tradesman of a corpulent and respectable appearance, with habiliments somewhat ostentatious, were to slide down gently into the mud, and dedecorate a pea-green coat, I am afraid we should all have the barbarity to laugh. If his hat and wig, like treacherous servants, were to desert their falling master, it certainly would not diminish our propensity to laugh; but if he were to fall into a violent passion, and abuse everybody about him, nobody could possibly resist the incongruity of a pea-green tradesman, very respectable, sitting in the mud, and threatening all the passers-by with the effects of his wrath. Here, every incident heightens the humour of the scene—the gaiety of his tunic, the general respectability of his appearance, the rills of muddy water which trickle down his cheeks, and the harmless violence of his rage!
But if, instead of this, we were to observe a dustman falling into the mud, it would hardly attract attention because the opposition of ideas is so trifling, and the incongruity so slight.

In Sydney Smith's dissertation on humor, it must be conceded that, although himself a brilliant wit, he was, of course, referring to humor of the sort we would today describe as of the slapstick kind, but humor nonetheless. Within his illustration of wit and humor surely lies their essence, that is, the masterly use of *the opposition of ideas* combined with incongruity sometimes juggled into aphorism, epigram, paradox, situation—what you will.

There were many before and after Sydney Smith who had grappled with a desire to define wit. John Lyly in *Euphues: The Anatomy of Wit*, 1579, had pondered long on the challenge. "I have ever thought so superstitiously of Wit, that I fear I have committed idolatry against wisdom," he admitted.

"Many disagreed with La Bryére who, in *Characters*, in 1688, had testily held that "Impertinent wits are a kind of insect which are in everybody's way and plentiful in all countries. . . ." There's room for doubt there, but perhaps Lucretius, in the first century B.C., got fairly close to the truth in his essay "On the Nature of Things:" "In the midst of the fountain of wit there arises something bitter, which stings in the very flowers."

On a nationalistic basis, there *has* to be a combination of wisdom and wit which persuaded the celebrated de Goncourt brothers, Edmond and Jules, to strike in their *Journal*, 1858, a sardonic home run: "A delicate wit is a corruption which a nation takes a long time to acquire. It is only worn-out nations that possess it."

The same is probably true of people, as Hazlitt would have agreed. For was it not the erstwhile William who, in his *Lectures on the English Comic Writers*, 1819, summed it up so graphically, "Wit is the salt of conversation, not the food. . . ."? And as for the food in certain London clubs—and the Atheneum in Pall Mall, in particular—Wilde mused delightfully, "Ah, the Atheneum, where they understand all the arts and sciences with the exception of gastronomy."

In 1885, Oliver Wendell Holmes, in his *The Autocrat of the Breakfast Table*, tried hard—"The wit that knows his place is at the tail of a procession." But that processional placing would not have appealed to Oscar, always himself a front-runner. For his was invariably wit in plentitude. And he must be given the last word in terms of a story concerning *The Importance of Being Earnest.*

Unknown to the theatrical company, he had watched a performance of his play. Afterwards, he went backstage and called the company together. They feared a bombshell of criticism; instead, Oscar stood before them, elaborately attired in browns, fawns, and tans. He pronounced,

> My dear, delightful company, I have just watched your performance and I wanted you to know that it reminds me of a play I once wrote. . . .

FOR THE USE OF THE YOUNG

> *Fame has also this great drawback, that if we*
> *pursue it we must direct our lives in such a*
> *way as to please the fancy of men, avoiding*
> *what they dislike and seeking what is pleasing*
> *to them.*
> —BARUCH SPINOZA
> *On The Correction of the Understanding, 1677*

At the height of his acclaim, Wilde was understandably the recipient of many requests to perform favors for others. Some of these came from influential people within his circle of friends, others from his contemporaries at Trinity and Oxford.

In the early autumn of 1894, Frank Harris, who had become the editor of the *Saturday Review*, wanted a challenging circulation-booster. He approached Wilde who promised to help. Wilde promptly produced *Phrases and Philosophies for the Use of the Young*, a set of satirical "commandments." He had hardly finished writing them when he was asked by another friend, an Oxford contemporary, to lend a hand in the launching of a new Oxford magazine, *The Chameleon*, designed for distribution to undergraduates.

With characteristic generosity, Wilde handed over *Phrases and Philosophies for the Use of the Young*, with the intention of writing another piece for Frank Harris. He made no inquiries as to the content, format or purpose of the undergraduate publication.

The contribution was charmingly acknowledged by John Bloxham, the youthful editor of *The Chameleon* who told Wilde that his piece would lead the editorial content of the first issue. Lead the content it did, with Bloxham himself contributing a somewhat tasteless and, many claimed, blasphemous story, "The Priest and the Acolyte," which was the final story in the first number, December 1894.

There can be little doubt that Wilde read "The Priest and the Acolyte" because it is known that he received and returned a proof of the magazine, but at the time he made no protest. Perhaps he treated the proof cursorily?

In any event, it was only when Jerome K. Jerome, the distinguished author of *Three Men in a Boat* and other successful works, reviewed the first issue of *The Chameleon* in his own journal, *Today*, that trouble began. Jerome attacked as "thoroughly objectionable" the overall content of the magazine, singling out for especial bile the story, "The Priest and the Acolyte." He conveyed his disgust, too, to John Sholto Douglas, the intemperate Marquis of Queensbury.

Wilde made a vigorous protest to Bloxham. As a result, the issue was speedily withdrawn and the magazine sank without a trace. It should be stressed that Wilde had nothing to do with the editorial content beyond contributing *Phrases and Philosophies for the Use of the Young*. It is on record, however, that when he did read—or reread—"The Priest and the Acolyte" he was appalled at the treatment of a sensitive subject, although he may well, as has been suggested, have agreed with the subject material.

As far as his own *Phrases and Philosophies for the Use of the*

Young were concerned—"wisdom," they were described, "in a witty form"—at no time did he regret having penned these. They were, in essence, an assortment of Wildean aphorisms, epigrams and other axioms—"innocuous and cynical sophistries," the author described them. Wilde, in fact, at his delightful best.

However "innocuous" in concept, they were later to cause him many disturbing moments, at which time he was to defend them with a diverting display of devastating verbal pyrotechnics. Even today most *Phrases and Philosophies for the Use of the Young* remain unequaled in their Wildean gaiety and blunt, satirical "truth," as these examples show.

THE FIRST DUTY in Life is to be as artificial as possible. What the second duty is no one has as yet discovered.

WICKEDNESS is a myth invented by good people to account for the curious attractiveness of others.

IF THE POOR only had profiles there would be no difficulty in solving the problem of poverty.

THOSE WHO SEEK any difference between soul and body have neither.

A REALLY well-made buttonhole is the only link between Art and Nature.

RELIGIONS die when they are proved to be true. Science is the record of dead religions.

THE WELL-BRED contradict other people. The Wise contradict themselves.

NOTHING that actually occurs is of the smallest importance.

DULLNESS is the coming of age of seriousness.

IN ALL unimportant matters style, not sincerity, is the essential.

IN ALL important matters, style, not sincerity, is the essential.

IF ONE tells the truth, one is sure, sooner or later, to be found out.

PLEASURE is the only thing one should live for. Nothing ages like happiness.

IT IS ONLY by not paying one's bills that one can hope to live in the memory of the commercial classes.

NO CRIME is vulgar, but all vulgarity is crime. Vulgarity is the conduct of others.

ONLY the shallow know themselves.

TIME is a waste of money.

ONE SHOULD always be a little improbable.

THERE IS a fatality about all good resolutions. They are invariably made too soon.

THE ONLY WAY to atone for being occasionally a little overdressed is by being always absolutely overeducated.

TO BE premature is to be perfect.

ANY preoccupation with ideas of what is right or wrong in conduct shows an arrested intellectual development.

AMBITION is the last refuge of the failure.

A TRUTH ceases to be true when more than one person believes in it.

IN EXAMINATIONS the foolish ask questions that the wise cannot answer.

GREEK DRESS was in its essence inartistic. Nothing should reveal the body but the body.

ONE SHOULD either be a work of art, or wear a work of art.

IT IS ONLY the superficial qualities that last. Man's deeper nature is soon found out.

INDUSTRY is the root of all ugliness.

THE AGES live in history through their anachronisms.

IT IS ONLY the gods who taste of death. Apollo has passed away, but Hyacinth, whom men say he slew, lives on, Nero and Narcissus are always with us.

THE OLD believe everything: the middle-aged suspect everything: the young know everything.

THE CONDITION of perfection is idleness; the aim of perfection is youth.

ONLY the great masters of style ever succeed in being obscure.

THERE IS something tragic about the enormous number of young men there are in England at the present moment who start life with perfect profiles, and end by adopting some useful profession.

TO LOVE oneself is the beginning of a life-long romance.

Without doubt, Oscar himself embraced, in fullness and objectivity, the final tenet of his published "Philosophies."

A CARD—AND A WRIT

*Scandal is the offspring of envy and malice—
nursed by society, and cultivated by disappointment.*

—Countess of Blessington (1789-1849)

Academics, legal luminaries, and others who have studied
the ill-fated life and trials of Oscar Wilde are unanimous in
the opinion that Wilde himself brought about his own downfall. Is this precisely true?

What would any man—let alone a genius like Wilde—be
expected to do as the recipient of a barrage of villification,
insults, libels, and harassment such as Wilde endured at the
hands of Lord Queensbury, who stopped at nothing to put an
end to Wilde's friendship with his son, Lord Alfred? Bosie,
gifted though he was (and we have Lord Birkenhead's testi-
mony that he was "a brilliant boy"), regarded his father with a
psychopathic loathing that was tantamount to blind hatred:

this hatred was known to consume the boy long before he met Wilde, and not without reasons.

Queensbury was determined to wreck the reception of Oscar's play *The Importance of Being Earnest*, but was thwarted in doing so by George Alexander, who refused the nobleman seats for the first night. Not to be outdone, Queensbury deviously tried to penetrate the theater carrying a "floral arrangement" of turnips and carrots, which he intended to present to the author at the start of his first-night speech. But all doors were barred against the Marquis on Alexander's orders. Consumed with anger, he left St. James's, depositing Wilde's edible bouquet at the stage door with "His Lordship's Compliments."

Queensbury then threatened to disown Bosie completely unless he stopped seeing Wilde. Bosie responded by sending his father a telegram retorting, "What a funny little man you are!"

All this, and Queensbury's enmity within the social salons of London, seemed insufficient to content the hate-wracked Marquis. His anger was not dissipated by the anonymous publication of a satirical story, "The Green Carnation," plainly based on the Wilde-Bosie Douglas friendship.

Lord Alfred begged Wilde to prosecute his father. Although sorely tried by the virulent and damaging campaign, Wilde chose for the time being to ignore it. Together with Douglas, he went off on holiday to Algiers.

On his return, Oscar finally decided that enough was enough. The Marquis had called at his club, the Albermarle, in Dover Street, Piccadilly, contemptuously leaving an 'open' card with the hall porter addressed, "To Oscar Wilde—posing as a somdomite." The hall porter, embarrassed to leave the card lying around with its bad spelling and libelous content, placed it in an envelope, which he properly addressed to Oscar Wilde, Esquire, leaving it in the club's message box in the normal way.

On receiving the card, Oscar Wilde straightaway got in touch with Robert Ross, inviting him to call on him. He told Ross, "I don't see anything now but a criminal prosecution. My whole life seems ruined by this man . . . it is intolerable to be dogged by a maniac."

Most of Wilde's friends, among them Ross, More Adey, Reggie Turner, and Harris, tried to discourage him from taking legal action, but Bosie, "the graceful boy with a Christ-like heart," nagged Wilde to proceed. They talked far into the night. The next day Wilde acted. A writ was served on "The Scarlet Marquis" for criminal libel, returnable at Marlborough Street Police Court on 3 March. Only three days had elapsed since Wilde had received the card.

Queensbury's appearance at court was formal and brief. He was committed for trial at the Old Bailey, a *prima facie* case having been made out, as required by English law. He was released on bail with £500 surety.

Queensbury seemed unconcerned at the turn of events. Wilde, he considered, had taken his bait. He went to his barrister friend, George Lewis, who, out of his own friendship to Wilde, refused to take the case. Queensbury then turned to Charles Russell, a well-known solicitor of his time. Russell agreed to act for him and without delay sought to brief Edward Carson—"Coercian Carson"—Wilde's contemporary at Trinity. Carson, gifted and diligent, brilliant in cross-examination, balked at taking the brief, feeling that he could not appear for Queensbury against 'his fellow alumnus'; he also considered that there was little defense in Queensbury's case.

Undaunted, Russell did not brief another counsel; instead he employed private detectives, giving them a directive to seek further evidence with which to nail Wilde. By the most fortuitous stroke of luck, Russell's men happened across precisely the evidence he needed.

One of Russell's detectives chanced to call at a London West End shop that, unknown to him at the time, was being watched by the police who were seeking to prove that the place was—in Victorian terminology—"a house of ill-repute." The detective got into conversation with one of the tarts, who vehemently complained of business being abysmally bad. Upon inquiring why, the detective met with a torrent of obscene invective against one Oscar Wilde who, the tart claimed, was responsible for the appalling competition from homosexuals that she and her kind were experiencing.

The detective egged her on. The tart told him to visit a certain address where, he was assured, he would find all the evidence he needed against Wilde. Acting on the information, the detective found exactly what he needed: a mailbox containing names and addresses of lower-class youths with notes "indisputably" connecting them with Wilde.

Charles Russell returned to Carson's chambers and presented counsel with the damning evidence. Still, Carson was reluctant to appear against Wilde. His dilemma was great. He decided to seek the opinion of Lord Halsbury, a recent and highly-respected Lord Chancellor. "What must I do?" he asked Halsbury. "You must arrive at justice," said the Law Lord, "and it is you, I believe, who can best do it." Thus, Carson was finally persuaded to accept the brief.

When Wilde heard that Edward Carson was to appear for Queensbury at the Old Bailey trial, he was highly amused, telling his friends with marked good humor, "I am to be cross-examined by old Ned Carson." Wilde well knew his adversary and seemed delighted at the turn of events. Carson, he believed, was no match for him; Carson's knowledge of literature and life was minuscule beside his own. He might well have been right about Carson's lack of appreciation of his kind of literature, but he was to be proved abysmally wrong about Carson's knowledge of life.

For much of the waiting period, Wilde socially was at his brilliant best, entertaining many friends, disseminating laughter wherever he went. The trial began on 3 April 1895 and received huge publicity. The satirists and cartoonists had a field day.

Wilde arrived at the Court accompanied by Bosie. They sat together behind Oscar's imposing array of legal luminaries; for Wilde, no less a leading counsel than the avuncular Sir Edward Clarke, Q.C. M.P., ex-Solicitor-General, with Charles "Willie" Matthews as junior (later to become Sir Charles Matthews, D.D.P.), and Mr. Travers Humphreys (destined to become one of England's most eminent judges), as a second "junior" barrister.

Appearing for Queensbury, the defendant, were Carson, leading; Charles Gill, a brilliant advocate; and Gill's brother, Arthur, who was to become an outstanding police magistrate. Edward Besley, Q.C. and J. L. Monckton held watching briefs on behalf of Lord Alfred Douglas and his brother, Lord Douglas of Hawick.

Wilde looked across the packed courtroom at Edward Carson and smiled broadly. Carson, it is recorded, returned the smile by "looking coldly past the writer." Somebody broke the tension with a jovial remark about "the importance of being early."

The usher's traditional three knocks at the door of the courtroom echoed through the dirty, colorless Old Bailey building.

Mr. Justice Henn Collins, the presiding judge, looking somewhat "Gilbert and Sullivan" in scarlet and ermine, entered, followed by the High Sheriff of London in court dress complete with sword, the City Clerk, and other dignitaries. Everybody bowed ceremoniously.

The judge took up the traditional bouquet of flowers, smelled them as his predecessors had done as a symbolic disinfectant against the Great Plague of London three hundred years before. The public and press galleries were packed to suffocation.

The Marquis of Queensbury stepped into the dock. The charge was read to him. In a clear voice, the nobleman pleaded "not guilty"; his counsel adding that "the words were true and published in the public interest." The stage was set for the trial—*Wilde v. Queensbury.*

Wilde's leading counsel, Sir Edward Clarke, had decided to rely on his client's plea of "complete innocence." Clarke wanted a fast and simple, clear-cut conviction of Queensbury on the single issue of criminal libel. Sir Edward chose his words carefully and attacked with cold precision, later calling on Wilde to give evidence.

Wilde, the celebrity and dandy, the bon vivant and social lion, looked immaculate, albeit (for him) soberly dressed. He rose, cool and urbane, giving his age as thirty-nine. At this, Carson looked up quickly, making a fast note.

Wilde was questioned about a man named Allan who had found a letter Wilde had addressed to Lord Alfred Douglas in a suit Bosie had given to the man. Allan, it appeared, had tried to blackmail Wilde. "A very curious construction could be put on that letter," Allan had said at the time, to which Oscar had replied, "Art is rarely intelligible to the criminal classes." But the blackmailer had persisted, "A man has offered me £60 for it."

Wilde, with bland reassurance, reminded the court that he

had told the blackmailer, "If you take my advice you will go to that man and sell it to him for £60. I myself have never received so large a sum for any prose work of that length, but I am glad to find that there is someone in England who considers a letter of mine to be worth £60!"

The court was beginning to react with amusement to this suave, engaging personality. Oscar had, it seemed, had further fun at the expense of the blackmailer. "I am afraid you are leading a wonderfully wicked life," he had said, to which Allan, on leaving, had replied, "There is good and bad in every one of us!" At this, for good measure, Wilde had shot back, "You are a born philosopher!" Wilde, with characteristic generosity, had then apparently taken pity on the wretch and given him money—ten shillings.

As Marjoribanks, a Member of Parliament, legal essayist, and biographer, later observed, "The man who could pay blackmail and laugh at the blackmailer at the same time was a very rare creature." But was ten shillings payment of blackmail?

Wilde claimed that the letter in question was nothing less than a work of art in itself, translated as it was by a French poet, Pierre Louÿs.

Questioned by his counsel about "The Priest and the Acolyte" in *The Chameleon,* Wilde agreed that the story was "bad and indecent," that he had no direct association with it and, when he discovered its inclusion, had been responsible for stopping publication of the undergraduate magazine.

Finally, Sir Edward asked his client—quietly and pointedly—as he had earlier asked him in the privacy of his chambers, "You are aware of the defense plea and the names of the persons with whom your alleged conduct has been impugned. Is there any truth in these allegations?" The reply was fast, direct and unequivocal. "There is no truth in any of them."

That evening, Wilde was to give further evidence of his

acute sense of self-mockery. While crossing Regent Street, he met an actor of his acquaintance, Charles Goodhart. The street was placarded with newspaper headlines about the case. Goodhart was clearly ill at ease, referring to the weather. Wilde smiled and went straight to the point, indicating the placard. "You've heard of my case, Charles? Please don't distress yourself. All is well. The working classes are with me . . . to a boy."

LAUGHTER IN COURT

*The essence of morality is the subjugation of
nature in obedience to social needs.*
 —JOHN MORLEY (1871-1908) "Carlyle," *Critical Miscellanies*

The court was now gearing itself for the confrontation of
the two ex-Trinity men: Edward Carson, Q.C. M.P., and Oscar Wilde, Hellenist, poet, and writer.

Carson rose slowly. Before him lay a copy of Wilde's birth
certificate. With considered deliberation he framed his first
question. "Please state your age." "Thirty-nine," said Wilde.
"You state that your age is thirty-nine. I think you are over
forty. You were born on 16th October 1854. Do you wish to
pose as being young?" inquired Carson, putting great emphasis on the word *pose*. "No." "That makes you over forty?"

Wilde's vanity had preened itself too far in his characteristic pursuit of youth. It was a small point, but a telling one.
He was quick to regain his mien. He smiled, raising his eyebrows in a half-longing gesture, and emitted a brief, yearning

"Ahh . . . ," as if mourning his lost youth. The court laughed, but was quickly silenced by the judge.

Carson then questioned Wilde on Lord Alfred Douglas's age; how long they had known each other; where they had stayed together.

He then turned to Wilde's association with *The Chameleon*, dissecting the prurient details. Wilde's attention was casual to the point of studied nonchalance. "I have only read it once, last November, I think, and nothing will induce me to read it again." "You are of the opinion that there is no such thing as an immoral book?" "Yes." "May I take it that you think "The Priest and the Acolyte was not immoral?" "It was worse—it was badly written!"

Wilde admitted that the story was "horrible and disgusting," but not, he claimed, "blasphemous." Then, with great emphasis, he leaned towards learned counsel, and studiedly emphasized, "I do not believe that any book or work of art ever had any effect on morality whatever."

Carson seemed momentarily jarred by the statement. Regaining himself, he asked, "So far as your work is concerned, you pose as not being concerned about morality or immorality?"

He repeatedly provoked Wilde with the word *pose*. Wilde, with airy assurance, replied, "I do not know whether you use the word *pose* in any particular sense?" Rejoined Carson, "But it is a favourite word of your own." "Is it? I have no *pose* in this matter!" Then, with an air of faint disdain, Wilde continued, "In writing a play, a book, or anything, I am certainly concerned with literature—that is, with Art. I aim, not in doing good or evil, but in trying to make a thing that will have some quality of beauty."

The courtroom was hushed as Carson turned his cross-examination to *Phrases and Philosophies for the Use of the Young*, each and every phrase of which he dealt with separately. His caustic delivery made them sound trite and shallow. But it was Wilde's opportunity to take command of the situation. "Listen, Sir," demanded Carson, " 'Wickedness is a myth invented by good people to account for the curious attractiveness of others'. You think that is true?" "I rarely think anything I write is true!" " 'Religions die when they are proved to be true.' Is that true?" "Yes, I hold that. It is a suggestion towards a philosophy of the absorption of religions by science, but surely it is too big a question for you to go into now," Wilde teased. "Do you think that was a safe axiom to put forward for the philosophy of the young?" "Most stimulating!" " 'If one tells the truth one is sure, sooner, or later, to be found out'?" continued Carson. "This is a pleasing paradox, but I do not set very high store on it as an axiom." "Is it good for the young?" persisted Carson. "Anything is good that stimulates thought, in whatever age."

" 'Pleasure is the only thing in life one should live for'?" "I think that the realisation of oneself is the prime aim of life, and to realise oneself through pleasure is finer than to do so through pain. I am on that point entirely on the side of the Greeks. It is a pagan idea."

" 'A truth ceases to be true when more than one person believes in it,' recited Carson. "Perfectly. That would be my metaphysical definition of truth; something so personal that the same truth could never be appreciated by two minds."

Carson was icily persistent. He continued, " 'The condition of perfection is idleness; the aim of perfection is youth'?" "Oh, yes. I think so," smiled Wilde. "Half of it is true. The life of contemplation is the highest life, and is so recognized by the philosopher."

Carson's Irish brogue was intruding. He took a further example. " 'There is something tragic about the enormous number of young men there are in England at the present moment who start life with perfect profiles, and end by adopting some useful profession'?"

Oscar smiled. "I should think that the young have enough sense of humor." "You think that is humorous?" persisted Carson. "I think it is an amusing paradox, an amusing play on words. . . ." Carson went doggedly on.

"What would anybody say would be the effect of *Phrases and Philosophies* taken in connection with such an article as 'The Priest and the Acolyte'?" "Undoubtedly it was the idea that might be formed that made me object so strongly to the story. I saw at once that maxims that were perfectly nonsensical, paradoxical, or anything you like, might be read in conjunction with it." There was a heavy pause.

Turning to *The Picture of Dorian Gray*, Carson suggested that a decadent construction could be put on the novel. "Only by brutes and illiterates," Wilde replied with assured *brio*. "But an illiterate person reading *Dorian Gray* might consider it such a novel?" Wilde was ready. "The views of illiterates on Art are unaccountable!"

Carson then speculated on the opinions of ordinary individuals of *Dorian Gray*. "I have no knowledge of the views of ordinary individuals," quipped the wit emeritus.

Shrewdly turning to the attitudes and views of the characters in *Dorian Gray*, Carson laid much emphasis on a character who "had adored another man madly." "Have you, sir, ever entertained such adoration?" he asked Wilde pointedly. "I have never given adoration to anybody except myself," retorted Wilde with a superior smile.

Despite the hilarity in court, Carson ignored the reply and turned to a letter from Wilde to Bosie Douglas. "What about this passage?" he asked." " 'I have adored you extravagantly. . . .' " "Do you mean financially?" joked Wilde.

For the first time, Carson displayed anger. His voice became steeped in aggressive irony. "Oh, yes. Financially. Do you think we are talking about finance?" he asked. "I've no idea what you are talking about!" replied Wilde. "Don't you?" parried Carson. "Well I hope I shall make myself very plain before I have done."

He proceeded to call into further allusive analysis the letter Wilde had written to Bosie. The court listened in silence, hanging on every word. Carson waited for Wilde's reply.

"I think it is a perfectly beautiful letter," said Wilde simply, adding, "You might as well cross-examine me as to whether a sonnet of Shakespeare is proper." "Apart from Art?" countered Carson. "I cannot answer apart from Art." "Suppose," questioned Carson diffidently, "suppose a man who was not an artist had written this letter, would you say it was a proper letter?" Back came the lightning retort, "A man who was not an artist could not have written that letter!"

Laughter filled the courtroom; even the judge's severe stare was seen to break into a half-smile. Wilde was a past master at playing to the gallery. And his friends were there in force— Ernest and Ada Leverson, Mrs. Bernard Beere, Frank Harris, Ellen Terry, Charles Wyndham, Adela Schuster, Lady Mount Temple, More Adey. . . .

The confrontation was at its height. Carson's crisp Irish accent, overlaid with his Dublin brogue, was now more pronounced than before, as he posed question after question. Each was answered by Wilde with the smooth, cultured tones of the *littérateur*. It appeared that "Coercion" Carson had more than met his match.

But Carson's solid reputation as a painstaking, persistent, and brilliant cross-examiner had not been built on hearsay; it had been well and truly established by accomplished performances in innumerable courts. He was by no means finished with his adversary in the witness box.

"Can I suggest," he asked quietly, "for the sake of your

reputation, that there is nothing very wonderful in this . . . 'red rose lips' phrase of yours?" "A great deal depends," said Wilde genially, with a dig at Carson's Irishness, "on the way it is read." "'Your slim, gilt soul walks between passion and poetry.' Is that a beautiful phrase?" "Not as you read it!" taunted Wilde. "But I do not profess to be an artist," countered Carson adroitly, adding for good measure, "and when I hear you give evidence, I am glad I am not!"

With cool deliberation, Carson shuffled his papers and produced a further letter from Wilde to the youthful Bosie. It was a lyrical, if not impassioned, exhibit. The barrister read it aloud with slow emphasis. Stopping, he toyed with the letter and asked, "Is that an ordinary letter, would you say?" Wilde was ready for the taunt. "Everything I write is extraordinary!" he replied with disarming conceit, adding, "I do not *pose* as being ordinary!"

Wilde had deployed his replies with consummate wit and skill, never for a second showing any sign of loss of temper. His delivery was precise, elegant, and crisp.

But the lean, pale-faced Irish advocate was now getting into stride.

It was late in the afternoon when Carson turned his attention towards a murkier area—"where the Poet of The Beautiful joined company with valets, grooms, and blackmailers in dim-lit, curtained, perfumed rooms. . . ."

Wilde repositioned himself in the witness box, displaying not the slightest trace of apprehension. Of course he mixed with all stratas of life. He was, after all, a lover of life. "And youth?" countered Carson scornfully. Surprisingly, Wilde agreed. Youth, to him, was inspirational, and he was a writer. "Why should my characters all come from affluent drawing-rooms?" he asked. So he had given the blackmailer Allan ten shillings for his trouble in attempting blackmail? "I gave it out of contempt," said Wilde forcibly. "Then your way to show contempt is by paying ten shillings?" "Yes. Very often," replied Wilde in his driest tone.

But had not Wilde, suggested counsel, invited *another* youth, who worked in a publisher's office, to a sumptuous repast in an exclusive restaurant? "Was that for the purpose of having an intellectual treat?" taunted Carson. "Well, for him—yes!" replied Wilde, to the high amusement of the court.

Clearly, Wilde, embattled, had fought his way brilliantly out of a series of heavily loaded legal questions, all deftly delivered by an accomplished and experienced advocate.

Carson looked cynically at Wilde and invited him to step down.

As Carson himself sat and began fingering through his formidable brief, Wilde remembered his words, "I shall make myself very plain before I have done."

The court adjourned until the next morning.

OBLOQUY OF A GENIUS

*The greatest fault of a penetrating wit is to go
beyond the mark*

—Duc de La Rochefoucauld
Maxims, 1665

The newspapers reported the court proceedings with a
sensational relish amounting to indecency. On the first day's
showing, Wilde had clearly been the victor—the humanist, the
brilliant poet and writer who seemed to care for the illiterate,
the underdog; a man of compassion who, although a sophisticated celebrity, elitist, and friend of the famous, could still
identify with the ordinary fellow, the man in the street. Several newspapers commented on Carson's bitter, sardonic
cross-examinations as almost amounting to open hatred. And
little less than that it was to prove next day.

Carson resumed his cross-examination, overwhelming
Wilde with relentless questioning relating to the perfumed
rooms as well as to an intellectual named Taylor who, Carson
claimed, had introduced Wilde to boys and youths in lowly

circumstances. He also referred to expensive presents and secret *rendezvous*. Carson's briefing solicitor and his investigators had done their work diligently and well. "What enjoyment was it to a man in your position," asked Carson accusingly, "to be entertaining grooms and coachmen?" Wilde shot back his reply, "The pleasure of being with those who are young, bright, happy, careless and original." Carson: "Had they plenty of champagne?" Wilde: "What gentleman would stint his guests?" Carson: "What gentleman would stint the valet and the groom?" he mimicked cuttingly.

The advocate then announced that he proposed to call a succession of witnesses to speak for themselves and for the edification of the jury. From this it was apparent that hereafter there would be scant further laughter in the courtroom, except that of derision as Carson recited the list of his witnesses and their occupation: grooms, valets, and coachmen. . . . For the first time, Wilde displayed signs of stress; his speech became hesitant, his lips were seen to tremble. Russell's field work had forced him into a corner from which he patently found it difficult to extricate himself.

Now came the advocate's final assault. With icy, clipped words, he asked, "Did you know a certain waiter who worked at a certain Parisian hotel?" Wilde screwed up his lips as if in pain. He hesitated. And hesitated yet again. Then, obviously distressed, he answered quietly that "Yes, he thought he would know the waiter. . . ."

It is now part of legal and literary history that Carson, with devastating brilliance, proceeded to attack Wilde again and again. It was the barrister's case that a man named Wood had stolen the letters from the suit to provide Allan, the blackmailer, with his evidence. Carson then claimed that Wood had been packed off to New York. Moreover, he accused Wilde, "You paid his fare! But," said Carson quietly," he did not to go New York; he is here and will be cross-examined."

Turning to the jury, he asked, "In view of these disgusting letters from Wilde to Lord Alfred Douglas, are you going to send Lord Queensbury to jail?"

He continued, "Bear in mind that Lord Queensbury's son is so dominated by Wilde that he threatened to shoot his own father . . . my client did what he has done most deliberately, and he is not afraid to abide by the issues in this court." Then, with assured and measured gesture, Carson indicated that Wilde could leave the witness box. It was all over . . . except the shouting.

What, the members of the court asked themselves, would Edward Clarke, Wilde's counsel, do to remove the stench of Carson's smearing cross-examination? After all, Wilde had brought the action; he was *not* the defendant.

Surely Clarke would put Lord Alfred in the witness box to testify against his father's unrelenting cruelties, not only to his wife and family, but to many of their friends—several of them famous names in the land. Queensbury's letters to his youngest son referring to his relationship with Wilde reeked of spite, malice, and hate. Surely Clarke would call Lord Alfred, whose evidence must clearly square matters once again in favor of Wilde? Most of the lawyers and officials in court had been convinced that Clarke had been holding Lord Alfred Douglas in reserve. But it was not to be. The "beautiful, accomplished boy" sat close to Wilde's side, mesmerized by the turn of events.

By the time the court adjourned, Wilde's own leading counsel was convinced of his client's guilt. How could he still proceed with the case? Charles Matthews, his junior, disagreed with his leader. It was their duty, Matthews averred, to fight the case to a finish. But if it proceeded, argued Clark quietly, Carson would call further damning evidence, a succession of hoydenish males of the lower orders.

If Wilde lost—as lose it seemed he now must—the judge had a duty to impound the papers and pass them straight to Hamilton Cuffe, the Public Prosecutor, who would then arrest Wilde and arraign him for another trial—this time as the accused.

Clarke immediately sought a conference with Wilde, who looked and behaved as if experiencing a bad dream; he seemed powerless of decision. But Clarke persuaded him on a course of action. The case continued into the next day.

It was a formality and neither Wilde nor Bosie were in court at the opening. Carson recited a list of the witnesses he now proposed calling, "young men more sinned against by Wilde than sinning."

> I have to bring before you each of these young men to tell their tales, for an advocate—a most distasteful task . . . after their evidence, you will wonder, not that gossip reached Lord Queensbury's ears, but that the man Wilde has been tolerated for years in Society as he has. . . .

A quick consultation took place between Carson and Clarke.

Sir Edward Clarke, somber and direct, rose and addressed the judge and the jury. "I am prepared to submit to a verdict of Not Guilty for Lord Queensbury," he said. "I trust, my lord, that this will bring an end to the case." The judge concurred. He addressed Sir Edward, "A verdict of Not Guilty means a complete justification of the whole plea, you understand?" Carson interrupted, "Then, my lord, the verdict will be that complete justification is proved and that the publication by my client was for the public benefit."

Wilde arrived at the Old Bailey late in the afternoon, having previously agreed with Clarke to abandon the case. He had been absent in order to prepare a statement for the press, which was released as he and Bosie arrived at the court:

It would have been impossible for me to have proved my case without putting Lord Alfred Douglas in the box against his father. Lord Alfred was extremely anxious to go into the box, but I would not let him do so. Rather than put him in so painful a position, I determined to retire from the case and to bear on my own shoulders whatever ignominy and shame might result from my prosecuting Lord Queensbury. . . .

Minutes after Lord Queensbury was discharged, a letter enclosing a heavy bundle of documents and depositions was despatched by messenger to the Director of Public Prosecutions in Whitehall.

Wilde and Douglas retired exhausted to a room in the nearby Holborn Viaduct Hotel. George Wyndham, Lord Alfred's cousin and a member of Parliament, arrived to warn Wilde to make haste to leave the country. A warrant for his arrest was at that moment being signed. Wilde, trembling and benumbed, refused to see him. He went instead to the Cadogan Hotel, Sloane Street, stopping off at a bank to collect a large sum of money. He was not aware that another carriage was following his every move.

While her son was at the Cadogan, Lady Wilde stood outside his Tite Street house supervising the removal of piles of luggage on to a waiting cab. As she did so, a newspaper boy turned into the street shouting the stop-press news, "Arrest of Oscar Wilde . . . Oscar Wilde Arrested!" Frank Harris had been right. They had arrested him.

Perhaps the most descriptive recall of the scene inside the Cadogan Hotel was penned by John Betjeman (now Sir John Betjeman, Poet Laureate) many years later. He commemorated the devastating day with a poignant poem, "The Arrest of Oscar Wilde at The Cadogan Hotel:"

> He sipped at a weak hock and seltzer
> As he gazed at the London skies

Through the Nottingham lace of the curtains
Or was it his bees-winged eyes?

To the right and before him Pont Street
Did tower in her newly-built red,
As hard as the morning gaslight
That shone on his unmade bed,

"I want some more hock in my seltzer,
And Robbie, please give me your hand—
Is this the end or beginning?
How can I understand?

"So you've brought me the latest *Yellow Book:*
And Buchan has got in it now:
Approval of what is approved of
Is as false as a well-kept vow.

"More hock, Robbie—where is the seltzer?
Dear boy, pull again at the bell!
They are all little better than *cretins,*
Though this *is* the Cadogan Hotel.

"One astrakhan coat is at Willie's—
Another one's at the Savoy:
But fetch my morocco portmanteau
And bring them on later, dear boy."

A thump, and a murmur of voices—
("Oh why must they make such a din?")
As the door of the bedroom swung open
And two PLAIN CLOTHES POLICEMEN came in:

"Mr. Woilde, we 'ave come for tew take yew
Where felons and criminals dwell:
We must ask yew tew leave with us quoitly
For this *is* the Cadogan Hotel."

He rose, and he put down the *Yellow Book*
He staggered—and, terrible-eyed,

He brushed past the palms on the staircase
And was helped to a hansom outside.

After he had assembled his papers, Carson left the court
and went down to the House of Commons. Moodily, he received repeated congratulations from his fellow Parliamen-
tarians. "Did you ever compete against Wilde at Trinity?"
someone asked. "I was never an infant prodigy," replied Carson laconically.

As the remark died away, workmen outside the Haymarket
and St. James's Theatres, where two of Wilde's plays were
running, stood perilously on ladders against the theater fa-
çades removing the name of Oscar Wilde from the credits of
The Importance of Being Earnest and *An Ideal Husband.* In
London and the big provincial cities, crowds gathered in the
streets, held hands and danced in derisive joy at the news of
Oscar Wilde's arrest.

During the three weeks between Wilde's arrest and the second trial, Queensbury petitioned the courts and successfully
made Oscar Wilde a bankrupt because of nonpayment of
costs. Wilde's beautiful house and its contents at Tite Street
were pillaged; he was stripped of all his possessions, which
were sold for minor sums at public auction.

During this time the Marquis of Queensbury was involved
in an ugly street brawl with another of his sons, Lord Percy
Douglas, in St. James's, which led to both being charged the
next day with disorderly conduct.

Wilde's second trial started on 20 May 1885. He was accused on a criminal charge of offenses against Section XI of
a then comparatively recent statute. The trial ended pre-
cipitately with the jury unable to reach a verdict. A retrial
was ordered by the court.

It subsequently became known that Edward Carson (destined to become Lord Carson) privately appealed for lie-

niency for Wilde. "Cannot we let up on the fellow now? He has suffered a great deal," he pleaded. But the law, geared for the kill, had to take its course, albeit without Carson prosecuting this time.

While awaiting his third trial, Wilde was given bail in the amount of several thousand pounds. His name was so enmeshed in mud and opprobrium that none would stand surety for him except, surprisingly, Lord Douglas of Hawick, Lord Alfred's eldest brother. There was a moment of infinite compassion when the young clergyman Stewart Headlam stepped forward, thus risking himself to a large fine if Wilde did not redeem his bail. The churchman gave as the reason for his action that "Oscar Wilde had shown beauty on a high hill. . . ."

During the third trial, Sir Edward Clarke—who this time charged Wilde no fee for his services—pleaded again for his client with a passion and sincerity not entirely characteristic of a lawyer in the High Court. But to no avail; this final trial culminated in a summing up of vitriolic invective by the judge, Mr. Justice Wills, who, in his conclusion, sentenced Wilde "to be imprisoned and kept to hard labour for two years." It lay within his power to bind over, or put under legal bond, the accused man and so satisfy the law, but Judge Wills chose not to take this humane course.

Such is the irony of fate and "man's inhumanity to man" that on the same evening of Oscar Wilde's terrible obloquy two of the leading actors in *An Ideal Husband*, Charles Hawtrey and Charles Brookfield, who both loathed the playwright, gave a celebratory dinner for the "heroic" figure of the Marquis of Queensbury, while enjoying the employment and rewards afforded them by Wilde and his genius.

George Bernard Shaw, in a reluctant Postscript to the rascally Frank Harris's *Life of Oscar Wilde*, remembered,

I was ordinarily acquainted with Wilde's reputation, but until he prosecuted Queensbury I had never heard a word about his homosexuality and, further, the late Carlos Blacker, an intimate friend of Wilde, told me that he also had not the faintest suspicion of anything of the kind and was as amazed as I was when it came to light.

More than sixty years later, it was left to St. John Irvine, a distinguished British literary critic and author (not, it should be said, a person given to praising Wilde or his works) to write of Queensbury, "The Scarlet Marquis" in a published polemic,

A more unholy scoundrel never defiled the earth by his presence on it. The Marquis of Queensbury was either the embodiment of evil who should have been destroyed, or an incurable lunatic who should have been certified and secluded. . . .

Many, many years later, Travers Humphreys, Wilde's second junior barrister at the trials, by this time a Knight of the British Realm and a learned High Court judge, gave his opinion of the case. He wrote in his memoirs,

Reflecting on the events, one fact is plain beyond argument. The prosecution of Oscar Wilde should never have been brought.

THE DAY OF THE LABURNUM
AND THE LILAC . . .

All fame is dangerous: good bringeth envy;
bad, shame!
—THOMAS FULLER, M.D., *Gnomologia*, 1732

They took him to Holloway Gaol, transferring him later to Wandsworth Prison, in South London, and still later to Reading Gaol. En route to Reading, in Berkshire, Wilde was to undergo the awful indignity of publicly waiting on a platform at Clapham Junction railway terminus handcuffed to his guards while onlookers derided him.

Even the revered and freethinking Professor Mahaffy, he of Oscar's Trinity days, heeded the crowing of the cocks as he deserted his one-time brilliant classical scholar. By this time Sir John, he answered all inquiries with, "We do not mention the name of Mr. Oscar Wilde."

There is little need to dwell on the devastating effect the trials, the resultant publicity, the unseemly arrest, and the degradation of the sentence had on this gifted man, except to record that he served his harsh sentence with "noble servility." If there was any laughter left in his being, it must have been shatteringly hollow. As Sydney Smith had earlier and ironically remarked in the 1800s, "Toleration never had a present tense. . . ."

It is part of literary legend that, while incarcerated, Wilde wrote his mystical and moving apologia in the form of a lengthy letter to Lord Alfred Douglas, *De Profundis: (Epistola: In Carcere et Vinculis)*. An exquisite exposition of sensitive writing, parts of it were, perhaps understandably, an impeccably phrased indictment of Bosie.

> I allowed you to dominate me, and your father to frighten me. I ended in horrible disgrace. There is only one thing for me now—absolute Humility: just as there is only one thing for you, absolute Humility also. You had better come down into the dust and learn it beside me. . . .

If his apologia contained bitterness, it was a bitterness that was to pass. He continued with a beautifully observed examination of his future.

> All trials are trials for one's life, just as all sentences are sentences of death, and three times I have been tried. . . . Society, as we have constituted it, will have no place for me, has none to offer; but Nature, whose sweet rains fall on unjust and just alike, will have clefts in the rocks where I may hide, and secret valleys in whose silence I may weep undisturbed. She will hang the night with stars so that I may walk abroad in the darkness without stumbling, and send the wind over my footprints so that none may track me to my hurt; she will cleanse me in great waters, and with bitter herbs make me whole. . . .

De Profundis was not simply an indictment of Bosie. It was—and remains—a lucid, emotional explanation; coherent and mystical, vividly understandable to artists, then and now.

It was in no sense a defense except, perhaps, for his words, "I surrounded myself with smaller natures and with meaner minds," and, "What the paradox was to me in the sphere of thought, perversity became to me in the realm of passion," if anything an indictment of *himself* engendered by the remorse of retrospection.

The fates, who seem never to take kindly to what today is described as "a loser," had not finished with Oscar Wilde. He had lost his good name, all his beautiful possessions—and his freedom. Yet abject unhappiness was still to be his lot.

In the early spring of 1896 his wife, Constance, traveled from Genoa, Italy, to see him at Reading Gaol. There she broke the news to him of his mother's death. His deep affection for Jane Wilde had remained constant over the many years of struggle and success, and Oscar was temporarily overtaken by consuming grief. He knew that his ignominious trials and subsequent imprisonment had hastened her end—she who had always adored him and had basked in his popularity and success.

What did Constance herself think of her husband's calamitous situation? In a letter of 26 March 1897 to her brother, she wrote, "I think his fate is rather like Humpty Dumpty's, quite as tragic and quite as impossible to put right." She had effected a deed of separation from him, agreeing to pay him £150 a year provided he avoided seeing Bosie Douglas. But he was deeply wounded by the condition that he would not see his sons.

Yet, even in his obloquy, there were still those—and some in Reading Gaol itself—who held or retained a respect for his genius. Not least of these was the prison governor, Major J.O.R. Nelson, who, within the limits of "stretched" regulations, did much to make part of Oscar's incarceration bearable.

Nelson passed on to the Home Office each of Wilde's three

separate petitions for a review of his severe sentence. These had no effect; but the governor, out of compassion, did "unofficially" provide him with jail-embossed paper on which he was to pen his last prose work, *De Profundis.*

The early months of Oscar's imprisonment filled him with unabated horror and depression. Time was to mellow this to a strange, cataleptic reconciliation with his dire situation. Those around him noticed an occasional shaft of wit, a brief return to some of the warmth of his former personality, as when speaking of Queen Victoria, he wryly remarked, "If Her Majesty does not treat her prisoners any better, she does not deserve to have any."

Talking was strictly forbidden within the confines of the jail, but occasionally warders would exchange the odd word or pleasant remark with Wilde. One such was an uneducated soul who nonetheless sought to improve his scant knowledge of literature and writers by furtive contact with the prisoner. The warder would surreptitiously "arrange" little talks with Wilde. "Excuse me, Sir," he ventured one day. "Now Charles Dickens, would he be considered a great writer, Sir?" Oscar smiled gently and replied, "Oh, yes. A great writer indeed. You see he is no longer alive." "Yes, I understand, Sir. Being dead, he would be a great writer, Sir?"

On another snatched occasion, the warder asked Oscar about John Strange Winter.° "Would you tell me what you think of him, Sir?" "A charming person," replied Oscar, "but a lady, not a man. Not a great stylist, perhaps, but a good, simple storyteller." "Oh, thank you, Sir. I did not know he was a lady, Sir."

On yet another occasion, the same warder again called Oscar aside. "Excuse me, Sir, but Marie Corelli, would she be considered a great writer, Sir?" This was more than Oscar

---

° Mrs. Henrietta Stannard (1856-1911), who wrote under the pen name "John Strange Winter"

could bear. Putting his hand gently on the man's shoulder, he smiled kindly, "Now, don't think I have anything against her moral character," he said, "but from the way she writes, she's the one who ought to be here!" The warder was said to have looked askance. "You say so, Sir? You really say so?" Obviously, Wilde had not entirely lost his sense of humor!

The majority of Wilde's friends predictably failed him in his distressing circumstances, but there were the few who were constant in their friendship, notably Robbie Ross, for so long his loyal aficionado. Frank Harris was another visitor, as were More Adey, Reggie Turner, and Sir William Rothenstein. Shaw did not appear.

One or two of them believed they detected that Oscar was gradually reinvigorating some of his old literary powers. He talked to them of books, plays, and criticism, but he had abandoned as unfinished his two current works, *A Florentine Tragedy* ("Wisdom comes with winters") and *La Sainte Courtisane* ("Death is not a god. He is only the servant of the gods"). An interest in the literary scene, yes; but now was not the time for a return—if that be possible—to his accustomed literary and intellectual pursuits. And headaches were troubling him.

A small shaft of light unexpectedly penetrated the darkness of his world. Robert Ross conveyed to him the news that Lugne-Poe had staged *Salomé* in Paris. But even this event afforded him scant joy. He was still languishing within the caldron of mental distress; contemplation of loftier things in his ugly, oppressive circumstances and surroundings was not easily enjoyed. Inspiration is so often proscribed by circumstances; the writing of *De Profundis* had been an urgent imperative—a purging of the past.

To regret one's own experience is to arrest one's own development. To deny one's own experience is to put a lie into the lips of one's own life. It is no less than a denial of the soul.

Yet, patently, there had to be regret of sorts; otherwise, why the groping pursuit for total humility? A personal inner search for sanctity and mental sanctuary was his insistent, recurring syndrome. "How else but through a broken heart may Lord Christ enter in?" he wrote. And,

> The important thing, the thing that lies before me, the thing that I have to do if the brief remainder of my days is not to be maimed, marred, and incomplete, is to absorb into my nature all that has been done to me, to make it part of me, to accept it without complaint, fear, or reluctance. . . .

Could there be any sort of future? There was at least the hopeful vista of eventual freedom.

> I tremble with pleasure when I think that on the very day of my leaving prison, both the laburnum and the lilac will be blooming in the gardens. . . . Like Gauthier, I have always been one of those "pour qui le monde visible existe."

Wild, the poet, as opposed to Wilde the sophisticate, was a true Celt, a romantic whose romanticism he dared not reveal, except perhaps in his fairy stories, "The Happy Prince" and "A House of Pomegranates." He loved the cadenced prose of his language; his self-imposed condition of that prose had been simply that it must always be beautifully expressed.

Now the hoped-for return of the wit and sophisticate must optimistically await the day of release, the day of the return of the laburnum and the lilac. . . .

FREEDOM, FRANCE, AND
AN ENCOUNTER WITH CARSON

*Fame is but an inscription on a grave, and
glory the melancholy blazoned on a coffin lid.*
—ALEXANDER SMITH
"On The Writing of Essays"
Dreamthorp, 1863

The lilac and laburnum blossomed. On 18 May 1897, Oscar Wilde, felon, was secretly removed from Reading Gaol to Pentonville, the forbidding North London prison from where he was set free during the early hours of 19 May. He had been transferred from Reading overnight because rumor had reached the Home Office that there might be a demonstration outside Reading by some of Queensbury's associates.

In spite of the prison rules to the contrary, governor Nelson had handed Oscar his manuscript, *De Profundis*. Outside the huge, gothic gates of Pentonville, the faithful Robbie Ross awaited his friend. Without a word, Oscar handed the manuscript to him, and together they left the oppressive shadows of the gaunt prison. They went to the Reverend Stewart Headlam's house to meet Ernest and Ada Leverson.

That night, in company with Ross and Reginald Turner, Wilde traveled to the coast and boarded a ferry steamer to Dieppe, France, where they registered at the Hotel Sandwich. He was never to return to his adopted homeland.

Defeated and intimidated by his awful imprisonment, he had temporarily changed Ross's name to Reginald Turner and Turner's to Robert Ross. As for himself, he had decided that henceforth he would be known as Sebastian Melmouth, a name taken from a book written by a relative of his.

Almost his first move in France was to write a lengthy and brilliant appraisal of the prisoner's lot, the cruelties, indignities, and abject demoralization to which those in prison were perpetually subjected. He sent it to a London newspaper, which published it without altering a word. It was this moving appeal that brought about a new Parliamentary Act which initiated previously unheard-of reforms in British prisons.

The little party of three stayed in Dieppe for close to three weeks. Oscar, slowly returning to his normal self except for acute headaches, felt again an urge to work. He moved quarters to the Hôtel de la Plage in a small village called Berneval on the northern coast of France. A month or so later he took a modest house, the Chalet Bourqeat, in the center of the village. It was here that he wrote *The Ballad of Reading Gaol*, his celebrated and moving exposition of "Death and Dread and Doom."

> I know not whether the Laws be right,
> Or whether Laws be wrong;
> All that we know who lie in gaol
> Is that the wall is strong;

And that each day is like a year,
A year whose days are long. . . .

Ross and Turner returned to London. Oscar continued to write in loneliness and recurring sadness. But the creative gift had all but disappeared.

His depressions were suddenly and unexpectedly eased when Lord Alfred Douglas, whom Oscar had sworn never to meet again, arrived in Berneval; "the beautiful boy" of whom, a year or two later, Wilde's old acquaintance, T.W.H. Crosland, was to address in a sardonic sonnet beginning "You were a brake and more than half a knave. . . ."

Within days, Oscar and Bosie left the Berneval village house for Posilipo, Naples. By taking up his friendship with Bosie again, Oscar thus forfeited his allowance.

Prison had taken its full toll of the Master. The bouts of sickness which had overtaken him in jail—a sickness of excruciating headaches and nausea, with a legacy of spells of recurring black depression—scarcely ever left him, the result of a fall in Wandsworth prison that had necessitated an ear operation. The realization that he could never return to his former eminence consumed Oscar's entire being. Soon his creative bent left him altogether.

His sickness—a condition that throughout his life he had loathed in others and feared in himself—was crushingly heightened by more bad news. Constance, his wife, had died at Genoa. He wanted to see his sons, but her family refused his request. He went to stay with Harris at La Napoule, just along the coast from Cannes, then moved thence for a while to Lake Geneva.

Two years after his release from prison—two years to the exact month—he moved back to France and took what for him were ugly rooms in the Hôtel d'Alsace on the Rue des Beaux-

Arts. The landlord, Jean Dupoirier, proved an understanding friend. He stayed there for little over a year and a half, leading an aimless existence, the while suffering from ever-increasing head pains, the hurt of which now consumed most of his waking hours. At this tragic juncture a strange incident occurred—an incident that in its macabre way had the same touch of terror as the final pages of *Dorian Gray*.

It happened in the winter of 1900.

Edward Carson, now at the height of his legal and parliamentary career and perhaps Britain's most distinguished legal luminary, was spending a few days in Paris. The skies were leaden and rain was beginning to fall when the advocate went out for a short walk. He stepped off the pavement at the same moment that the driver of a Parisian horse-drawn *fiacre*, with the Parisian drivers' usual lack of concern, thundered towards him, all but running him down. Rain had started to lash the pavements, and Carson's clothes were splattered with mud.

As he stepped back quickly on to the pavement, he clumsily butted into a man behind him who, on the impact, fell to the ground. Carson turned, stooping apologetically to assist the unfortunate victim. For a fleeting second, their eyes met. Carson stared into the haggard, pained features of Oscar Wilde, his ex-classmate those long years ago at Trinity, Dublin, the man he had ruined. "I beg your pardon," said Carson quietly. The bedraggled figure of Oscar Wilde, ignoring the lawyer's profuse apology, raised himself and walked on into the Parisian twilight.

Carson must have remembered that scene ruefully in the weeks that followed. There, in the gutter, had fallen the genius who, at his zenith, had invented and delivered a succession of the most brilliant paradoxes, aphorisms, axioms, and maxims ever conceived in the English language. There, gaunt and ill, was the one-time most celebrated conversationalist of the entire London social scene. There, old before his years, was the past arbiter of style, the accomplished Hellenist, playwright, bon vivant, and—yes—Lord of Laughter, the genius who had said or written,

For he to whom the present is the only thing that is present, knows nothing of the age in which he lives.

It is enough that our fathers have believed. They have exhausted the faith faculties of the species. Their legacy to us is the skepticism of which they were afraid.

The only thing that consoles man for the stupid things he does is the praise he always gives himself for doing them.

When you convert someone to an idea, you lose your own faith in it.

Extravagance is the luxury of the poor, penury the luxury of the rich.

The true artist is known by the use he makes of what he annexes, and he annexes everything.

To have a style so gorgeous that it conceals the subject is one of the highest achievements of an important and much-admired school of—leader-writers!

It is only the intellectually lost who ever argue.

You can't make people good by Act of Parliament.

Experience is a question of instinct about life.

The gratitude of most men is but a secret desire of receiving greater benefits.

Everyone is born a King and most people die in exile.

Lamentably there was no deus ex machina to descend like a winged chariot from the heavens above his personal stage to tie up the loose ends of his life, loose ends that hung like painful, raw nerves, wracking his being with memories of achievement and a world of unfulfilled promise. There was no perceptible future, only the ignominies of the past.

Wilde's random peregrinations across France and Italy, usually paid for by one or two of his remaining friends, gave him scant inspiration to continue with his writings. But, shortly before he died, London and Paris were surprised by the unexpected news that Frank Harris had apparently written a play called *Mr. and Mrs. Daventry*. It was further announced that the great Mrs. Patrick Campbell would present the play as well as appear in the role of Mrs. Daventry. Harris preened himself as the opening night approached; but it soon became the talk of London that Oscar Wilde had co-authored the play.

News of this reached the ears of Mrs. Pat. She tackled Harris about the authorship, especially when she was assailed by other managements who claimed already to have bought the same play from Wilde. And the fur, we are assured, flew! As Vincent Brome remembers, "Wilde appears, in his desperate and despairing straits, to have sold the idea of the play many times over!"

Certainly Wilde and Harris had earlier stayed together in Paris, and, as we know, Oscar had been Harris's house guest at La Napoule. There seems little doubt that Wilde had supplied Harris with the scenario, or story line, for the project, and much of the dialogue had a Wildean sharpness.

While the controversy raged, no word was heard from Wilde. Meanwhile, Harris was up to his old tricks losing no time in trying to persuade Mrs. Pat to become his sleeping partner. Although she had a reputation of attracting her leading men to her bedchamber, Harris apparently had no appeal for her in this direction.

The play was well cast; beside Mrs. Pat, Fred Kerr played Mr. Daventry, and Gerald du Maurier, Mrs. Daventry's lover, with an actor named George Arliss in the role of a comic waiter. It opened at the Royalty Theatre, London, on 25 October 1900, attended by Wilde's old friend the Prince of Wales, who, within a matter of months, was to become the King of England. In the first two acts, in particular, the play boasted "a bountiful display of those pyrotechnics which were the charms and weakness of *The Importance of Being Earnest*." The theatergoing public, indignant and cant-ridden, poisoned to the name of Oscar Wilde, reacted in a manner that seemed to spell doom for the play. It was widely alleged that Harris "had lent his name to another man's deed"—Wilde's.

But critics like the powerful Jack Grein found the play "extremely interesting," although Max Beerbohm in the *Saturday Review* likened Harris, the alleged author, to

> a bull in a china shop—horns to the floor, hoops in the air, tail a-whirl, the unkindly creature charges furiously hither and thither, and snap! crash! bang! into flying smithereens goes the crockery of dramatic laws and conventions, while the public lies quailing under the counter. . . .

The play came off after fifty performances, was rewritten, and reopened with Max Beerbohm's curtain-raiser, *The Happy Hypocrite*, preceding it. It closed for the two-week period of public mourning for the death of Queen Victoria and reopened at the start of 1901.

After a short period, it sank into virtual oblivion, although Mrs. Pat never lost faith in it. Many years later she tried to stage it again with the New York Theater Guild, and there was talk of it becoming a film. But both projects came to naught; the play was never performed in America. To her credit, throughout the American negotiations Mrs. Pat insisted that Wilde's name be shown as co-author with Harris on all publicity.

Mr. and Mrs. Daventry has never appeared in any published list of the works of Oscar Wilde.

HALF SAINT, HALF SATYR?

Since when was Genius found respectable?
—ELIZABETH BARRETT BROWNING (1816-1861)

Wilde's aversion to any form of illness, either in himself or in others, was not fear but a reflection of his deep-rooted compassion for those who suffered. That is the view of those who knew him best. It is difficult to equate this with the popular image of the hedonist whose life seemed to be one of unrelenting self-indulgence, plus an acid wit often exercised at the expense of others. Yet, we know that throughout his life he was drawn towards religion—especially at low points: while in prison writing *De Profundis,* as well as just before his death. Indeed, throughout his halcyon period, seldom a day had passed without his picking up a Bible; sometimes he would read it for a few hurried minutes between engagements, at others he would shut himself in his study in silence with the Scriptures for hours at a time.

It certainly could not be said of Wilde that he would have shared the view of one of the later presidents of Trinity College, Oxford, who, when asked what the four statues on the top of the church tower represented, absentmindedly replied, "The Holy Trinity." "But there are four," voiced an objector. "Of course," the president exclaimed, "three persons and one God!"

Wilde wasn't either to hear the delicious story of his once-beloved Professor Mahaffy. According to Dr. Oliver St. John Gogarty, Mahaffy was taken aback when approached by a Bible-thumping zealot who, cornering him in a railway carriage, demanded to know, "Are you saved?" "To tell you the truth, my good fellow, I am," replied Mahaffy, "but it was such a narrow squeak that it does not bear talking about!"

Wilde had always been fascinated by Jesus Christ, the man, and had written—but not published—a good deal of short, strange, evocative sidelights on His life, work, and charismatic character. Many of Oscar's close friends had testified and paid tribute to his intellectual affinity with the Son of God and his sensitivity towards the supernatural. In one of his short religious pieces, Oscar had written,

And He passed out of the city, and saw an old man weeping by the wayside, and asked him why he wept. The old man answered "Lord, I was dead and you brought me back to life. What else can I do but weep?"

This was another, unexpected side of Wilde, the man who, according to many of his friends, was said to possess pronounced mystical powers to aid the distressed and the sick. There were, too, those who testified to his considerable curative gifts. It was acknowledged that he could bring about a transformation of the physical condition through changing the mental attitude of others. How he did this is not precisely known, but there are some interesting examples on record.

His power was described by the Reverend Stewart Headlam as a "precious supernatural gift," and by Robbie Ross as "an uncanny but potent benefaction." Lord Alfred Douglas, too, is on record as saying, "One could meet him feeling abjectly depressed. Within five munutes, by his concentrated talking, he could change one's entire approach to a problem when everything became the color of a rose." In an exceptional way, his dominant personality and caring nature seemed to have a healing effect on the sufferings of others.

Walter Sickert's mother was prostrated with grief at the loss of her beloved husband. She refused to leave her bedroom. When nothing others said or did seemed to help her, the painter in desperation asked Oscar to call.

When Oscar arrived at the house, Sickert's mother flatly refused to see him. Wilde asked Sickert to leave him alone in a room, where he remained in silent contemplation for a full five minutes. Then, walking straight into the bedroom where Mrs. Sickert lay sobbing uncontrollably, Wilde took her gently by the hand and, without a word, helped her to a chair, where he sat down beside her. Her daughter, who was with her, quietly withdrew from the room.

Oscar and the elderly Mrs. Sickert were alone where they stayed together for a long time. The daughter later recorded, "Suddenly, I heard my mother laughing joyously. When Oscar left, she was a woman transformed, and she stayed that way. . . ."

Frank Harris had been confined to his rooms for some days, feverish and depressed. On hearing this, Wilde hurried to see him and remained for over an hour. That night the fever left the journalist, and he was back at work two days later, telling his friends, "Oscar, for all his fickle ways, is a miracle man. . . ." A tribute indeed, from a man not normally given to embracing the verities of life.

And the wealthy man-about-town Graham Robertson, wretchedly nursing a heavy cold and suffering a violent toothache also, refused all callers. Ignoring this, Oscar arrived, *insisted* on seeing his friend, and started talking. Within half an hour, Robertson, whose toothache quickly left him, sat down to a hearty meal with Wilde, the two of them in hilarious mood throughout the meal. "For what is religion but the supernatural regulated?" argued Gogarty, adding, "Magic deals with eternal values. . . ."

It could, of course, be said that Wilde's Irish temperament, his legendary kindness, Celtic insights, and sympathetic manner induced a like attitude in others by the power of positive thought. Whatever the truth, the result was often little short of amazing.

William Morris, enduring a protracted illness before his death, claimed that the only person he would allow to see him was Wilde. "Indeed," recorded Morris, "I was never so entertained in my life. He injected happiness into one's being. The impression left . . . by Wilde's nature is one of innate virtue."

Wilde, having moved to France after his debilitating trials, stayed for a while at the Hôtel des Bains, La Napoule, with the ubiquitous Frank Harris, then moved to Gland, near Lake Geneva, where he was the houseguest of the strange, hedonic Harold Mellor. He did not particularly like Mellor and made his excuses to return to Paris.

One day, when Wilde called at the Café de la Paix for an aperitif, actress Ada Rehan, with her manager, Augustin Daly, and his wife, were dining at a nearby table. In spite of his rejection by many of his friends, he was asked to join the group and, according to the actress, "The dinner proved enchanting for all concerned."

Four days later, Augustin Daly suddenly collapsed and died. Ada Rehan recalled that she "felt" Oscar was the only person who could help the inconsolable widow. She contacted Wilde, who hurried to Daly's wife, a totally bewildered woman, shattered at the sudden death of her husband. Ada explained, "I was at a total loss as to know what to do. Oscar was wonderful," she added. "He was like a kind, kind brother to the two of us—helpless women, as we were. He had this remarkable gift, the gift of penetrating solace combined with infectious laughter; it 'lifted' both body and soul." Ada Rehan was speaking of the man who, himself, had endured, and was still enduring, unceasing pain, mentally and physically.

At Mellor's insistence, Wilde returned to Gland but, after only another month with his host, moved to Rome. The celebrity now fallen from grace sought and received the Pope's blessing at the Vatican no less than seven times. A different Wilde indeed. Prison had confirmed to him that calamity was the lot of all great artists, that disaster was the healer, the cleanser of the inner Augean stable.

Yet, with his customary wit, he admitted, "Heaven is a despotism. I shall be at home there. . . ."

Half saint, half satyr? A good question.

THE LAUGHTER OF DEATH

We should live and learn; but by the time
we've learned it's too late to live.
—CAROLYN WELLS (1869-1942)

Wilde kept up a desultory correspondence with his few remaining friends in England. In a letter to More Adey dated 12 May 1897, he summarized his opinion of Frank Harris.

In fact, Frank Harris has no feelings. It is the secret of his success. Just as the fact that he thinks that other people have none either is the secret of the failure that lies in wait for him somewhere on the Way of Life.

Prophetic words? After Oscar's death, Harris, too, was to serve a sentence in prison. As also was Bosie—for libeling Winston Churchill.

Oscar was not reticent in telling Harris directly what he

thought of him. A month after his letter to Adey, he wrote to Harris and did not mince his words.

> To survive one must have a strong brain, an assertive ego, a dynamic character. In your luncheon parties in the old days, the remains of the guests were taken away with the debris of the feast. I have often lunched with you in Park Lane and found myself the only survivor. . . .

To his everlasting credit, Sir Herbert Beerbohm Tree, ever ready to lend a hand to friends who had fallen on bad times, wrote to Wilde that he had heard he was having a difficult time. He enclosed a sizeable check with a letter in which he wrote,

> No one did such distinguished work as you. I do most sincerely hope that your splendid talents may shine forth again. I have a lively remembrance of your many acts of kindness and courtesy, and was one of those who devoutly hoped that misfortune would not submerge you.

Turn the pages of *The Collected Works of Oscar Wilde* and his inordinate wit tumbles out like a stream of glistening gems; emanations of the superb mind of the genius who even wrote of death with humor. Had he not penned in *Dorian Gray*, "Death and vulgarity are the only two facts in the nineteenth-century that one cannot explain away"? And by his own personal tragedy and suffering, had he not squared his own accounts? He provided his own answer: "In her dealings with man, Destiny never closes her accounts."

In a lighter vein he had joked, "One can survive everything nowadays, except death." Even at the height of his fame, he had sardonically professed, "I shall never make a new friend in my life, though perhaps a few after I die." And, at about the same time, on receiving a large medical bill, he amusingly and accurately observed, "Ah, well, then, I suppose I shall have to die as I have lived—beyond my means!"

This last was to prove a prophetic summing up of Oscar Fingal O'Flahertie Wills Wilde.

As he lay in his dingy Parisian bedroom in the Hôtel d'Alsace, he re-read, "I wrote when I did not know life; now that I do know the meaning of life, I have no more to write. Life cannot be written; life can only be lived. . . ."

Oscar was dying; he knew the end was perilously close. He had earlier written to Ross, "my throat is like a limekiln, my brain a furnace and my nerves a coil of adders. . . ." Robert Ross and Reginald Turner hurried to his side. Biting his fist at the unendurable pain, Oscar's face was twisted like a German gargoyle. "It is killing me," he said to his friends. On 29 November 1900, the dying man asked to be received into the Roman Catholic Church. This was arranged with quiet ceremony.

Oscar turned to Reggie Turner the following day and whispered, "Last night I dreamed that I was dining with the damned souls in hell." Turner, we are told, looked at him with great understanding and affection, smiled weakly, and said, "And I've absolutely no doubt that you were the life and soul of the party!"

The greatest conversationalist of his era lapsed into endless silence.

He, of all men, had lived as few before him—magically and majestically; he had scaled the heights and touched the stars. His tragic and dramatic descent had mentally caused the flames of a living hell to lick grotesquely at his feet.

The death certificate, dated 30 November 1900, baldly

stated: "Cerebral Meningitis." Three days later his three closest friends were at the burial of the mortal remains of Oscar Wilde at Bagneux Cemetery.

Robbie Ross, a martyr to his long, loyal, and troublous friendship with Wilde was, in years to come, to be asked what he would choose to have inscribed on his own gravestone. A not inconsiderable wit himself, and no doubt recalling his often stormy association with Oscar, Ross replied, "Here lies one whose name is writ in hot water!"

Nine years after the internment, as a result of the representations of his remaining family, in addition to Ross, Turner, Bosie, and a few others, Wilde's remains were removed from Bagneux and reinterred in the large Parisian National Cemetery of Père Lachaise, near the Seine. Here, many celebrated artists, including Frederic Chopin, Gertrude Stein, Alice B. Toklas, Sarah Bernhardt, and Nijinsky, lie around him. Oscar Wilde rests beneath a monument carved by his old friend, Sir Jacob Epstein. Looking at the large sculpture, one can almost hear an echo of Oscar's witty comment on graveyard statuary, "To me, the frock coat of the drawing-room done in Bronze, or the double waistcoat perpetuated in Marble, adds a new horror to death."

On Epstein's huge, rectangular tomb, there is a quotation in Latin from Job, followed by a verse:

> And alien tears will fill for him
> Pity's long, broken urn,
> For his mourners will be outcast men,
> And outcasts always mourn.

As today's tourists and classical students stand and gaze on the grave of Oscar Wilde, there will doubtless be those who will recall Wilde's own epitaph, spoken in conversation with Robbie Ross,

> When the last trumpet sounds and we are couched in our eternal porphyry tombs, I shall turn and whisper to you, Robbie, "Let's pretend we do not hear it!"

And there will be few who will forget Oscar's reference to the red-flock wallpaper in his bedroom: "Oh, God, that ghastly wallpaper—it is killing me. One of us *has* to go!"

His was laughter to the last.

EPILOGUE

There never was a greater enigma than Oscar Wilde. He reached the heights and kicked the fingers of those on the ladder behind him. He then metaphorically kissed those same fingers with the tenderness of a smile. To him the supremacy of uniqueness was all, and he was uniquely supreme.

Since his death, there's scarcely been an able literary figure who has not attempted comment, blame, defense, dissection, or analysis of or on some aspect of Wilde or his work. Too few have fully understood his controversial, dazzling brilliance.

Let him provide his own Epilogue to this book, taken from *De Profundis*, written between January and March 1897:

> The Gods have given me almost everything. I had genius, a distinguished name, high social position, brilliancy, intellectual

daring; I made art a philosophy and philosophy an art; I altered the minds of men and the colour of things; there was nothing I said or did that did not make people wonder. I took the drama, the most objective form known to art, and made it as personal a mode of expression as the lyric or the sonnet, at the same time I widened its range and enriched its characterisation; drama novel, poem and rhyme, poem in praise, subtle or fantastic dialogue, whatever I touched I made beautiful in a new mode of beauty; to truth itself I gave what is false no less than what is true as its rightful province, and showed that the false and the true are merely forms of intellectual existence. I treated art as the supreme reality, and life as a mere mode of fiction; I awoke the imagination of my century so that it created myth and legend around me; I summed up all systems in a phrase, and all existence in an epigram. . . .

ACKNOWLEDGMENTS

To all of the following authors, editors, and publishers, British, American, and Continental, living or dead, and to the various literary executors involved, I express my gratitude for providing or helping to provide either direct quotations used in the text or indirect background and reference material. In some cases the quotation or reference has appeared in more than one source; when this has occurred I have sought to acknowledge all.

In a work of this kind, ommissions and sometimes minuscule inaccuracies, like those fey, unaccountable wartime gremlins, have a disconcerting propensity of inexplicably appearing—"first you see them, then you don't!"—despite assiduous attention to detail. I hope I am not guilty of failing to give credit where due. If I have erred, my apologies are tendered, together with an undertaking to repair such ommissions or inaccuracies in future editions.

I have found the following works most helpful:

Oscar Wilde and His World by Vyvyan Holland (Thames & Hudson); *Oscar Wilde* by H. Montgomery Hyde (Eyre Methuen); *Frank Harris* by Phillipa Pullar (Hamish Hamilton); *An Evergreen Garland* by Vyvyan Holland (Cassell) and *A Lifetime With The Law* by A. E. Bowker (W.H. Allen); *The Café Royal Story* and *Parnassus Near Piccadilly*, edited by Leslie Frewin, respectively Hutchinson-Benham and Frewin; *The Parents of Oscar Wilde—Sir William and Lady Wilde* by Terence de Vere White (Hodder & Stoughton); *Oscar Wilde, A Critical Study* by Arthur Ransome (Cassell); *W. B. Yeats—Interviews and Recollections*, Vol. 1, edited by E. H. Mikhail (MacMillan); *Mark Twain At Large* by Arthur L. Scott (Henry Regnery, Chicago); *The Oxford Book of Literary Anecdotes*, edited by James Sutherland (Oxford University Press); *Thomas Moore's Letters and Journals of Lord Byron* by Lord Macaulay (John Murray); *Mr. Frewin of England* by Anita Leslie (Hutchinson); *The Splendid Pauper* by Allen Andrews (George G. Harrap); *Bernard Shaw* by Frank Harris (Gollancz); *A Paler Shade of Green* by Des Hickey and Gus Smith (Frewin); *The Life of Sir Edward Marshall Hall, KC*, by Edward Marjoribanks (Gollancz); *My Life and Loves* by Frank Harris (Richards Press, 1952) and *Other Men's Flowers* by A. P. Wavell (Jonathan Cape); *The Smith of Smiths* by Hesketh Pearson (Hamish Hamilton); *Reading for Insight*, edited by J. Burl Hogins and Gerald A. Bryant, Jr. (Glencoe Press, California); *The Way It Was With Me* by Gerald Hamilton (Frewin); *Max Beerbohm* by Lord David Cecil (Constable); *Bernard Shaw* and *Beerbohm Tree* by Hesketh Pearson (Metheun); *Sixteen Self Sketches* by Bernard Shaw (Constable); *Oscar Wilde* by John Greer Ervine (Allen & Unwin); *The Wildes of Merrion Square* by Patrick Byrne (Staples); *Oscar Wilde and His Mother* by Anne, Countess de Bremont (Everett); *The Artist As Critic* by Professor Richard Ellman (W.H. Allen); *The Standard Bibliography of Oscar Wilde*, compiled by Stuart Mason (Werner Laurie, 1914); *The Letters of Oscar Wilde*, edited by Rupert Hart Davis (Hart Davis) 1962; *The Complete Works of Oscar Wilde*, 15 Vols (Dawson); *My*

World of Theatre by Sir Peter Daubeny (Jonathan Cape); *Speranza* by Horace Wyndham (Boardman); *Whistler* by Stanley Weintraub (Collins, 1974); *Laughter and Applause* compiled by Allan M. Laing (Allen & Unwin); *De Profundis (Epistola: In Carcere et Vinculis)* with Introduction by Hesketh Pearson (Penguin Books); *A Book of Trials* by Sir Travers Humphreys (Heinemann); *The Life of Lord Carson* by Edward Marjoribanks, M.P., (Gollancz); *Rufus Isaacs, First Marquess of Reading, 1860-1914,* by his son, The Marquess of Reading, K.C. (Hutchinson); and *Thesaurus of Anecdotes* by Edmund Fuller (Dolphin-Doubleday, New York); *Truth,* January 2 and 16, 1890.

I gratefully acknowledge my debt to the late Sir John Betjeman for the use of his poem, "The Arrest of Oscar Wilde at the Cadogan Hotel," and his verse preceding the chapter "Regent Street Royalist."

I have also consulted Hesketh Pearson's *Life of Oscar Wilde* (Metheun); Robert Harborough Sherard's *The Life of Oscar Wilde, The Real Oscar Wilde,* and *Oscar Wilde* (Werner Laurie); *The Story Of An Unhappy Friendship* (Greening, 1909); as well as Frank Harris's *Oscar Wilde, His Life and Confessions* (Constable); Vyvyan Holland's *Son of Oscar Wilde* (Hart-Davis); *Lempriere's Chronology;* and many books of quotations published in Britain and America, all of which I have found useful for checking purposes, but which would be too lengthy a list to recite here.

Special thanks are tendered to the editors of *Punch* magazine, the London *Observer, Sunday Times, Daily* and *Sunday Telegraph, The New York Times, The New Yorker,* and many state newspaper editors throughout America, not to mention the various kindly librarians in many American states and districts too numerous to detail.

I owe, too, deep gratitude which, sadly, I am unable to convey except by warm remembrance, to my late friends Captain Vyvyan Holland and Michéal Mac Liammóir, neither of whom once denied my probing of their prodigious knowledge of Oscar Wilde and his world.

LESLIE FREWIN
Kent, England, 1980

THE PUBLISHED WORKS
OF OSCAR WILDE

PLAYS

La Sainte Courtisane
A Florentine Tragedy
The Duchess of Padua
Vera, or The Nihilists
Salomé

The Importance of Being Earnest
An Ideal Husband
A Woman of No Importance
Lady Windermere's Fan

STORIES

The Picture of Dorian Gray
Lord Arthur Savile's Crime
The Model Millionaire

The Sphinx Without A Secret
The Canterville Ghost

FAIRY TALES

The Remarkable Rocket
The Devoted Friend
The Selfish Giant
The Nightingale and the Rose
The Happy Prince

The Star-Child
The Fisherman and His Soul
The Birthday of the Infants
The Young King

POEMS

POEMS IN PROSE

The Teacher of Wisdom   The Disciple
The House of Judgment   The Doer of Good
The Master   The Artist

DE PROFUNDIS AND ESSAYS

The Portrait of Mr. W. H.   Pen, Pencil and Poison
The Soul of Man Under Socialism   The Decay of Lying
The Critic as Artist   De Profundis

PHRASES AND PHILOSOPHIES FOR THE USE OF THE YOUNG

INDEX

Ayckbourn, Alan, 73
Aynesworth, Allan, 145

Balcombe, Florence, 101
Balfour, Arthur, P.M., 58
Ballad of Reading Gaol, The
    (Oscar Wilde), 131, 148, 201
Balzac, Honoré de, 104, 111
Bancroft, Squire, 83
Bankhead, Tallulah, 94
Barrie, Sir James, 84
Beardsley, Aubrey, 12, 77, 98, 123
Beecham, Sir Thomas, 94
Beecher, Henry Ward, 23
Beerbohm, Max *(Happy
    Hypocrite, The)*, 12, 60, 83,
    93, 122, 123, 206
Beere, Mrs. Bernard, 15, 182
Bennett, Arnold, 94
Berkeley Gold Medal (Classics
    Award, Trinity College,
    Dublin), 5
Bernhardt, Sarah, 10, 74, 77, 101,
    116, 216
Besley, Edward, Q.C., 174
Betjeman, Sir John *(Arrest of Oscar
    Wilde at The Cadogan Hotel,
    The)*, 92, 189
Bierce, Ambrose *(Devil's
    Dictionary, The)*, 116
Birkenhead, Lord, 170
Bishop, Alfred, 139
Blacker, Carlos, 193
Blessington, Countess of, 73, 170
Blind, Raffery *(County of Mayo)*,
    137
Bloxham, John *(Priest & The
    Acolyte, The)*, 166
Blunt, Wilfred Scawen, 45
Bok, Edward W., 97
Bomb, The (Frank Harris), 31

Boyle, Andrew (Tr. Spinoza's *On
    The Correction of the
    Understanding)*, 165
Bradshaw *(Bradshaw's Guide)*, 36,
    57
Bright, R. Golding, 25, 36
Brighton, Sussex, England, 97
Brome, Vincent, 205
Brookfield, Charles, 192
Brough, Fanny, 139
Browning, Elizabeth Barrett, 3
Browning, Robert, 121
Burden of Itys, The (Oscar Wilde),
    131
Burnand, F. C. *(Colonel, The* and
    Ed. *Punch)*, 10
Burns, Robert, 26

Cadogan Hotel, London, England,
    189, 190
Café Royal, The, Regent Street,
    London, England, 28, 30, 40,
    52, 59, 77, 92, 93, 94, 95, 96,
    97, 98, 99, 114, 115, 119, 120,
    123
Campbell, Mrs. Patrick, 205, 206,
    207
Canterville Ghost, The (Oscar
    Wilde), 102
Carson, Lord Edward Henry, Q.C.
    M.P., 6, 127, 172, 173, 174,
    175, 178, 179, 180, 181, 182,
    183, 184, 185, 186, 187, 188,
    191, 192, 203
Chameleon, The, 165, 166, 176,
    179
Characters (La Bryére), 163
Chesterton, G. K., 94
Chickering Hall, New York, 17
Chopin, Frédéric, 130, 216